You can!

Other Books in the Minirth Meier New Life Clinic Series

The Anger Workbook
Dr. Les Carter, Dr. Frank Minirth

Don't Let the Jerks Get the Best of You
Dr. Paul Meier

The Father Book
Dr. Frank Minirth, Dr. Brian Newman, Dr. Paul Warren

The Headache Book
Dr. Frank Minirth

Hope for the Perfectionist
Dr. David Stoop

Imperative People
Dr. Les Carter

Kids Who Carry Our Pain
Dr. Robert Hemfelt, Dr. Paul Warren

The Lies We Believe
Dr. Chris Thurman

Love Hunger: Recovery for Food Addiction
Dr. Frank Minirth, Dr. Paul Meier, Dr. Robert Hemfelt, Dr. Sharon Sneed

Love Hunger Action Plan
Dr. Sharon Sneed

The Love Hunger Weight-Loss Workbook
Dr. Frank Minirth, Dr. Paul Meier, Dr. Robert Hemfelt, Dr. Sharon Sneed

Love Is a Choice
Dr. Robert Hemfelt, Dr. Frank Minirth, Dr. Paul Meier

Love Is a Choice Workbook
Dr. Robert Hemfelt, Dr. Frank Minirth, Dr. Paul Meier

Passages of Marriage Series
New Love
Realistic Love
Steadfast Love
Renewing Love
Transcendent Love
Dr. Frank and Mary Alice Minirth, Drs. Brian and Deborah Newman, Dr. Robert and Susan Hemfelt

Passages of Marriage Study Guide Series
New Love
Realistic Love
Steadfast Love
Renewing Love
Transcendent Love
Dr. Frank and Mary Alice Minirth, Drs. Brian and Deborah Newman, Dr. Robert and Susan Hemfelt

The Thin Disguise
Pam Vredevelt, Dr. Deborah Newman, Harry Beveryly, Dr. Frank Minirth

Things That Go Bump in the Night
Dr. Paul Warren, Dr. Frank Minirth

The Truths We Must Believe
Dr. Chris Thurman

For general information about Minirth Meier New Life Clinic branch offices, counseling services, educational resources, and hospital programs, call toll free 1-800-NEW-LIFE.

You can!

Dr. Frank Minirth
with
Mark Littleton

THOMAS NELSON PUBLISHERS
Nashville • Atlanta • London • Vancouver

Published in Nashville, Tennessee, by Thomas Nelson, Inc.,
Publishers, and distributed in Canada by Word Communications, Ltd.,
Richmond, British Columbia.

The Bible version used in this publication is THE NEW KING JAMES
VERSION. Copyright © 1979, 1980, 1982, Thomas Nelson, Inc.,
Publishers.

Library of Congress Cataloging-in-Publication Data

Minirth, Frank B.
    You can! / Frank Minirth with Mark Littleton.
      p.   cm.
    ISBN 0-8407-7749-3
    1. Success—Religious aspects—Christianity.   2. Self-confidence
—Religious aspects—Christianity.   I. Littleton, Mark R., 1950-
II. Title.
BV4598.3.M56   1994
248.4—dc20
                                      94-27191
                                         CIP

Printed in the United States of America.
1 2 3 4 5 6 — 99 98 97 96 95 94

Contents

10.9

90054

You can!

PART ONE

Don't Give Up

CHAPTER 1

You Can—If You Believe You Can

In November 1988 my daughter, Renee, was diagnosed with diabetes, the disease I had fought all my life. I had hoped my children would not inherit it, even though I knew the odds were against us.

"Her blood sugar is 324," my wife, Mary Alice, sobbed over the phone. My heart sank then—and her words still reverberate today in the corridors of my mind.

Renee, who was ten years old, had been feeling weak, so Mary Alice had taken her to our pediatrician for an evaluation. I had prayed, "Oh, God, don't let her have diabetes; don't let her go through what I had to go through." But the high blood-sugar level confirmed my fears: Renee had diabetes mellitus, a chronic endocrine disease that requires a strict diet and daily shots of insulin.

My mind quickly flashed to scenes of my own childhood.

I developed diabetes at age twelve, and once I almost died from its complications. I still remember old Dr. Rodman's words: "Keep talking to him; let's keep his breathing going. Don't let him drift off to sleep," he told my mother over and over.

"Don't worry, Doc; I'm not going to die. There's too much fight in me," I responded.

I did survive and did fair at times, poor at other times. I remember the humiliation of being so sick when all my friends were so healthy. I remember having to take shots daily. I remember the extreme discipline of never being able to eat what I wanted. I remember the rejection of my friends who didn't understand why I couldn't eat candy and all the other junk foods they enjoyed.

Searching for every piece of the latest data about this disease, I talked to Renee's doctor, who specialized in diabetes, and to his nurse. Finally the nurse said, "Dr. Minirth, you are out-of-date; time has passed you by."

I didn't believe her at first, but a little neurosis slipped in. "What do you mean?" I asked.

The nurse continued, "Dr. Minirth, you are not on the latest type of insulin, Humulin N. You've had diabetes for over thirty years, but you have not recently been tested for injury to your kidneys. You're probably spilling proteins."

Spilling proteins, I thought apprehensively. In a few minutes this nurse had managed to slip some powerful doubts into my brain. *Out-of-date. Time has passed me by. Spilling proteins.* Anxiety about my own health added to my intense concern for Renee.

"All right, I will try the new insulin," I said. "I will test for the proteins. Surely, you're right. I'm probably dying!"

She just laughed, but I really felt worried. Then I did test for the proteins and I was fine. What a relief! Still, I tried the new insulin—and almost killed myself. It was a shock to my system and clearly something I couldn't tolerate.

Mary Alice told me, "Frank, you're not out-of-date. Time has not passed you by. You're as healthy as a horse. You're just becoming a little neurotic." With that little twinkle in her eye, she added, "If anyone's going to beat the odds, it's you. Remember your motto: You can if you believe you can."

From that time on, the idea would nag at me now and then, but I felt okay. Time had not crept up and taken my life away. I could fend off all those little neuroses that are planted in our heads by our doctors, lawyers, and friends. But my most important concern was still unsolved: Renee's health. Could new drugs save her from the pain I had suffered?

I read every new article describing medical research on diabetes, a condition partially related to an immune disorder in which the body begins to attack and destroy the beta cells of the pancreas. Some researchers in Canada had found that suppressing the immune system early on so it doesn't destroy the cells causes the pancreas to again produce insulin. Even though a person would have to remain on immunosuppressant medications, the progress of the disease could be halted, maybe even cured. That was my hope.

I conferred with the best medical brains in America, and they concurred that the work was valid but not without some risk. In less than a week, Renee and I were on our way to London, Canada.

I remember flying into the airport. The plane bumped and thrashed in the turbulent wind, and snow was blowing all around us. Only a week before a plane had crashed. The tumultuous, threatening weather matched our mood. It was right before Christmas and our hearts were heavy, but we both felt we had to fight for this now or we'd never have another chance. *You can if you believe you can,* I told myself again and again.

The numerous tests and the medicine were all painful. I spent every day with Renee and then went back to the hotel at night. We looked for a verse that would give us hope and comfort, and we didn't have to look far. In Genesis 18 God promised Abraham that his wife, Sarah, would have a child, even though she was almost ninety years old.

Abraham naturally questioned Him, and God replied, "Is anything too hard for the LORD? At the appointed time I will return to you," God promised, "and Sarah shall have a son" (v. 14). Nothing was impossible for our Lord. Whatever happens He is in charge.

Renee and I spent that Christmas in Canada; we grew closer together. On Christmas Day we called Mary Alice and the girls, and we called my mother. I was praying for Renee; she was praying for me. We had a common problem, and we were trying to solve it as best we knew how. Renee became my best friend, and I became hers.

We returned home after two weeks and then had to go back to Canada several times, but the medicine did not work. We had given it all we had, and lost.

The circumstance was not without blessings, however. Renee and I continued to believe that while we did not know God's will, we still knew nothing is impossible with Him. In our family discussions, in our time alone, in our individual prayers, we soon concluded, "No, we have not lost. God wants us to go on in spite of this. There is a ministry for Christ here, and He wants us to carry it out. We will go on. We will fight back in a different way—with a healthy diet, consistent exercise, and a good attitude. We will beat the odds for Christ!" It was a kind of pep rally of the heart, I guess.

And Renee did go on to beat the odds. Our personal prescription—a healthy diet, consistent exercise, and a good attitude—worked. Renee is a beautiful, healthy young lady. Today, despite the pain diabetes has caused us, I can thank God that He worked in our midst, worked it for good, and once again proved to me that you can if you believe you can.

Another blessing came later that year when Mary Alice became pregnant with Allie. Mary Alice was forty-two, and I was forty-four. God's promise in Genesis 18:14 was truly meant for us.

OTHER ODDS AGAINST US

More important than the odds against us physically are the odds against us mentally and spiritually.

I was discipled and grew in Christ through a group called the Navigators. They emphasize the study of the Bible, Scripture memory, prayer, fellowship with other Christians, and Christ as the center, or hub, of one's life. When I left for graduate school, I asked for the name of someone who could continue to disciple me. I was given the name of Dan, a godly man who could help me grow in Christ.

However, when I reached graduate school, I found it quite difficult. I forgot about Dan and concentrated on my studies, trying to survive. In my third year of graduate school I was watching a group therapy session through a two-way mirror one day when I heard a young psychologist say, "We have been discussing the meaning of life today. It varies for each of us. For me, it is Jesus Christ."

It took tremendous nerve and commitment to say those words in a secular school. The young man had spoken with true courage, and everyone's mouth opened in amazement. *Who was this young psychologist?*

Then I remembered. He was the one the Navigators had told me about. He was Dan.

After the session ended, I introduced myself to him. In the next week we became friends. We did Bible studies together, had prayer breakfasts, and grew in Christ. He was a dauntless young man who loved Christ.

In a year or so Dan went to another graduate school to work on a degree in theology. However, the school was liberal and Dan lacked true Christian fellowship. The last news I heard was that Dan had decompensated to the point that he had lost everything and was homeless.

How could this happen to a man like Dan, a devout Christian? I knew the answer. It happens because the world is against us; tremendous forces of darkness are trying to do us in. The odds are stacked against us, and my dear friend had lost to those odds. I knew if it could happen to him it could also happen to me, so I began an intense search to understand how a man or woman can hold on to this principle: You can if you believe you can.

Have you ever felt as if the odds were against you?

As if those odds were so great you might as well give up?

As if you were drowning and you had already gone down twice and were about to go down for the third and final time? Maybe the bills were too high, the mortgage was due, one of the kids was sick—it can all be too much!

What can I say to you in those circumstances? With all my heart I say *don't give up!* Don't count yourself out yet! You're not defeated! You can beat the odds!

I believe the keys to surviving life's hardships lie hidden in seven principles of Christian living. In this book I offer you those seven principles for beating the odds:

- In Christ—you can if you believe you can.
- Support your life with the triangle of strength: the Bible, prayer, and the church.
- Take care of all of you.
- Know that God is with you.
- Never give up.
- Grow through defeat.
- See life from God's viewpoint.

All of these principles flow from the same theme: You can if you believe you can. I know they work. They have worked for me, and they have worked for thousands of individuals in our hospitals over the years. These principles can work for you also. Apply them and beat the odds! Through them you can not only survive, you can win and go on to serve God even more mightily than before.

These seven principles are described in the next seven chapters. Apply them. You can if you believe you can!

PART TWO

Seven Principles for Overcoming the Odds

CHAPTER 2

The Vine and the Branches

1 *In Christ, You Can If You Believe You Can*

One day as I was making rounds an old gentleman whom I always tried to encourage said one word to me: "Good-bye." That day he did not mean good-bye for the evening but good-bye forever. I was a young doctor in Dallas and, though inexperienced, I tried my best that afternoon to help him. But I could not break his will to die. He was old, had lost his family, and was determined to end his life.

Early the next morning (4:00 A.M.) a call came from the nurse: "Mr. Smith just died."

"Died!" I exclaimed. "There were no major medical problems; he had no cancer, no heart illness. How did he die?"

"Doctor, he just stopped breathing."

Many thoughts rushed through my mind, but one

kept nagging at me: *Could it be that the brain is far more powerful than I have ever dreamed?*

As the years passed I began to notice a definite pattern. Those patients who could grasp some hope, who could sense that through Christ they could get well, usually did! Those who viewed themselves totally as victims of circumstances did not.

THE POWER OF OUR MINDS

I knew from my research that if an individual had a close relative—a spouse or child or parent—who died, his or her chance of dying within the next year was increased sevenfold. Why? There was no medical explanation. Could it be that the mind, with its chemical messages and psychological injunctions, holds the very keys to beating or losing to the odds?

My experience as a psychiatrist has proven this philosophy. Many years ago I hospitalized a patient we'll call Mr. Jones because he felt he could no longer cope; he begged to be admitted to the hospital. After an intensive medical and psychiatric evaluation, I felt his depression had more to do with his character than his physiology. Nevertheless, he pleaded for an antidepressant. Knowing the power of the mind, I decided to try a little experiment.

I told him, "Mr. Jones, a new antidepressant has been invented that is supposed to be great. It is called Diatam. Let's go ahead and give it a try. It is supposed to work quickly."

The next morning on rounds, Mr. Jones was ecstatic. "I feel so much better. Thank you, thank you, for finally giving me that wonderful drug."

"Mr. Jones, that was a placebo, a pill that has no real chemical value. I lied to you yesterday. You just had a sugar pill."

Well, at first he was furious, but later he was able to forgive me and we both had a good laugh. Once again I was amazed by the power of the mind.

In another situation I saw this same phenomenon, only in opposite circumstances. A patient, Mr. Smith, told me, "I react to all antidepressants. I have tried several, but I just can't take them."

This time lab tests indicated a biological depression, but he refused to take the medicine that could help him. So I told him, "Mr. Smith, there is a new antidepressant that is supposed to be great. It is called Diatam. It is supposed to have hardly any side effects. Will you give it a try?"

After much encouragement he reluctantly agreed.

The next morning on rounds he said, "I told you I couldn't take that medicine. I feel horrible, dizzy, nauseated, weak, just sick in general. You shouldn't have given me that medicine."

"Mr. Smith," I said, "that was a placebo, a sugar pill. I wanted to illustrate a point."

He then went on to make several points to me in

not altogether friendly terms, but later he did take a true antidepressant and did very well. Once again my belief had been reinforced. The brain can work for us or against us. It can be a mighty friend or a formidable foe. As a result, I began to ask, What if Christ could also use our minds for His glory?

The annals of research are filled with examples of the mind's effect on the body. We know that Type A (aggressive, competitive, time oriented, angry) individuals are more prone to heart disease. We know that stress can be the precipitating factor of some types of cancer. And we know that through the autonomic nervous system and other pathways the mind can produce actual disease (called psychophysiologic disorders) and even kill. In fact, in many forms of disease it is impossible to separate out the mental component.

The mind can indeed be a powerful friend and a strong foe, and it can alter our physical and mental attitudes by altering our body's chemistry and our behavior.

THE MIND'S POWER TO ALTER BODY CHEMISTRY

For years, we wondered how Valium, an antidepressant drug that has the highest sales of any pharmaceutical in the United States, worked. Researchers believed that there had to be similar chemicals in the brain or this drug would not be able to attach to the receptors there, but they couldn't find them until a few years ago. Then scientific research discovered endorphins and enkephalins, chemicals that influence our moods, especially in the areas of pain and pleasure. We believe they are released by laughter, exercise, and belief.

On the other hand, researchers also have found that stress can alter the body's chemistry negatively. It happens through several pathways:

- The autonomic nervous system. (Stress causes it to give us a more rapid heartbeat or release more acid into our stomachs.)
- The endocrine system. (Malfunctions can lead to thyroid disease.)
- The standard neurotransmitters in the brain, including serotonin, norepinephrine, and dopamine. (This is the main way stress affects us. When the serotonin or norepinephrine level is depleted we become depressed. An altered norepinephrine level can cause us to become manic. When the dopamine level is altered we get psychotic.)
- The immune system. (Stress decreases the immune system so we cannot fight off disease as well.)
- The musculoskeletal system. (Stress causes it to become more tight and tense.)

What a lot of damage to our health from something we can so easily avoid!

Another method by which the brain can affect us is through our behavior.

BEHAVIOR-INFLUENCED RELEASES

The brain uses its monumental memory and organizational system to implement behavior that will ultimately result in what we desire. That desire might be a simple action (like not getting up in the morning) or an unconscious wish (like our desire to receive attention or punish ourselves for past behavior).

I've seen the brain influence our behavior and emotions in patients like Mrs. Becker, who had entered our hospital in a severe state of depression. I always ask patients several questions to identify the cause of their disorder, and I often confront them with their responsibility for their emotions. I said to Mrs. Becker, "What are you doing to make yourself depressed?"

She was astonished that I would even ask such a question. "What am I doing to make myself depressed? I don't know what you are talking about."

"Mrs. Becker, there are no mistakes in life. Everything is planned out in great detail. Your brain often controls your actions. You could unconsciously be choosing to be depressed."

"I still don't know what you mean."

"For example, what time did you arise this morning?" I asked, explaining, "Most people who are depressed sleep late and then feel guilty for sleeping late."

"I arose at 7:00 A.M."

That was not abnormal. "What did you do then?" I asked.

"I got my children ready for school."

Again nothing abnormal. "What then?"

"Well, I hate to admit it, but then I went back to bed and I stayed in bed all day long."

That was the answer I had been looking for. So I probed further. "Do you get any exercise?"

"I don't even take my dog for walks anymore."

"Any social contacts?"

"I don't even go to church anymore."

"Anything else?" I asked.

"I hate to admit it, but I have been drinking a lot of alcohol."

"Alcohol produces a temporary euphoria but overall it is a depressant that only adds to your depression. Anything else?" I continued.

"Well, just before my husband gets home I get up, but I look bad."

"So all of this just happens to you?"

"No," she explained, "I did choose that behavior."

"Sure you did," I answered. "The brain sets up

behavior patterns to carry out the desired request. And that's why you're depressed."

GETTING TO THE HEART OF IT

James Allen said, "Let a man radically alter his thoughts and he will be astonished at the rapid transformation it will effect in the material conditions of his life."

We could take that quote and change it slightly: "Let a man begin to think he can do what he wants to do, and he will be astonished at the transformation it will effect in every area of his life."

And then we could take it one step further: "Let a Christian believe he or she can do something, and through the power and love of Christ it will surely be accomplished."

This principle—In Christ, you can if you believe you can—is not inner spiritual cheerleading. It's not mental hype. It's grounded in Scripture.

Jesus Himself said, "I am the vine, you are the branches. He who abides in Me, and I in him, bears much fruit; for without Me you can do nothing."[1]

He finished this thought by saying, "If you abide in Me, and My words abide in you, you will ask what you desire, and it shall be done for you."[2]

He didn't make that statement just once. He repeated it over and over again.

And at the Last Supper He told His disciples, "Most

assuredly, I say to you, he who believes in Me, the works that I do he will do also; and greater works than these he will do, because I go to My Father."[3]

The apostle Paul agreed with those powerful words. "I can do all things through Christ who strengthens me."[4] He didn't mean he could do anything—jump to the moon, solve all the problems on earth, lead every person to Christ, run a mile in two minutes, or rewrite the Old Testament—but he did mean that a realistic, prayed-through, Christ-supported, and purposefully pursued plan of action could be accomplished by anyone who would take those steps. In other words, if you believe you can, through Christ, you can!

One example I came across is from Y. A. Tittle, the great New York Giants quarterback in the 1950s and '60s. In 1947, Tittle was a quarterback on offense as well as a defensive back on the Louisiana State University football team. In one game against Vanderbilt he tackled a runner head-on and was knocked unconscious. The trainers dragged him off the field and stuffed ammonia under his nose. Blinking back to consciousness, Tittle heard the team doctor say he was out of the game.

Immediately, the line coach roared back, "Why?"

"The boy's hardly breathing," the doctor told the hard-nosed coach.

"You're the doctor!" the coach roared. "Make him breathe!"

Tittle didn't wait for the doctor to apply another healing touch. He jumped up, ran back into the game, and completed the next five straight passes!

Tittle is an example of one who could because he thought he could. I don't know that he connected those actions to a belief in Christ, but he was applying the principle. You can if you believe you can!

IS CHRIST NECESSARY?

That brings up the question, Is one's belief in Christ necessary for this principle to take effect? Certainly there are many examples from secular life where people who were committed to a cause or action have triumphed because they intuitively believed they could do it. Their conviction seemingly had nothing to do with Jesus, their faith in Him, or even an understanding of Scripture.

However, isn't Christ, regardless of an individual's personal relationship with Him, still Lord? Isn't it true that just as God can "[make] the plans of the peoples of no effect"[5] He also has "made all things for Himself"[6] and He "works all things according to the counsel of His will"?[7]

Certainly, the Christian has a special relationship with the Lord. Christ has committed Himself to us. He promises to make "all things work together for good"[8] in our lives as we love Him and follow Him. But not even non-Christians can claim that their success, achievement, position, or material wealth is purely of their own doing. It's like the husband who came home and proclaimed, "I'm a self-made man." His wife wisely answered, "You have just relieved the Lord of a tremendous responsibility!"

In reality, all that's good, just, right, decent, and worthwhile happens ultimately because God chose to make it happen. Just as Christ said in John 15:5, "Without Me you can do nothing," certainly no unbeliever can accomplish anything unless God allows him to. Even Epicurus, one of the Greek philosophers and certainly no Christian, said, "A strict belief in fate is the worst kind of slavery; on the other hand there is comfort in the thought that God will be moved by our prayers." Isn't that another way of saying that ultimately even the most pagan among us sooner or later realize they must invoke God's purpose and support to accomplish anything?"

I'm not teaching some kind of universalism or that one needn't believe in Christ. Please don't think that. No one can do anything to please God apart from faith in His Son.[9]

But in a larger sense, God has caused the world to function according to certain principles. Violating those laws leads to death both spiritually and physically. Living by those laws, however, will bring a certain degree of blessing from God. Paul said it this way in Romans 2:14, "When Gentiles, who do not have the law, by nature do the things contained in the law, these, although not having the law, are a law to themselves."

He told the Athenians on Mars Hill that, "He has made from one blood every nation of men to dwell on all the face of the earth, and has determined their preappointed times and the boundaries of their habitation, so that . . . they might grope for Him and find Him, though He is not far from each one of us; for in Him we live and move and have our being, as also some of your own poets have said, 'For we are also His offspring.'"[10]

At another time when the citizens of Lystra thought Paul and Barnabas were Greek gods, Paul told them, "We . . . preach to you that you should turn from these vain things to the living God, who made the heaven, the earth, the sea, and all things that are in them, who in bygone generations allowed all nations to walk in their own ways. Nevertheless He did not leave Himself without witness, in that He did good, gave us rain from heaven and fruitful seasons, filling our hearts with food and gladness."[11]

What Paul was saying was if a farmer who has no belief in Christ or even in the Creator, God, experiences success in his harvest, it is because God has blessed him. There is no other reason. If a man, woman, or child tries to grow a garden or run a race or make a profit in the market, he or she might falsely claim that any success is a result of his or her own efforts. But in reality, if God is not in it, that person will have achieved nothing.

A favorite story of mine is of Thomas Edison, who invented the light bulb. He had just completed his ten thousandth attempt to find the right filament that the electricity would not burn up. He went into the house and sat down, then shared this astonishing piece of news with his wife.

She asked, "Aren't you pretty discouraged, Tom?"

He replied, "Certainly not! Now I know ten thousand ways it doesn't work!"

Edison is considered the greatest inventor, not only in American history, but in the world. Again, his real spiritual status is unknown, but the question remains: Who was responsible for his success? Edison, himself, of course. He believed he could, and he did it. But behind him was Another who gifted him and undoubtedly subtly directed him to the resources that would make his inventions possible. Apart from God, no person, Christian or otherwise, can claim to have gotten the basic resources of success—intelligence, talent, ability, resourcefulness, or even the capacity to persist and hang in there. It's only one's own folly that tells a person he or she is a "self-made" man or woman.

Edison himself said that invention was "1 percent inspiration and 99 percent perspiration." But however much perspiration Edison shed, apart from God, he would not have had the gumption and desire to stick with the task through ten thousand failures. His ability was a gift of God.

That brings us to the issue of our own responsibility. However much we might believe God is the source of power, strength, skill, and understanding, we must also make the effort.

ASK, SEEK, AND KNOCK

I've always struggled with the balance between God's sovereignty and man's responsibility. How much of what we achieve depends on God, and how much depends on us? For every wildly successful person, there are probably a thousand ordinary folks who make no real mark in anything. What's the difference?

First, it's partly a recognition that God chooses to work *through* us, not just *for* us. Many mothers have told their children to "get up and go" because "God's not going to do it for you." The expression, God helps those who help themselves, is a much-criticized principle. However, to a large degree it is true. If Paul had not gone down to the port and booked passage on a ship, he would not have planted churches in Asia and Macedonia. Undoubtedly God would have raised up someone else.

All things in life require action, work, and effort. Yes, we must back it all up with faith, prayer, reliance on the promises of Scripture, and commitment to Christ, but to get anything done, we must take action.

I often hear Christians deride this idea. It's as though they expect God to work a miracle just for them. They think all they must do is pray and God will answer. But Jesus said, "Ask, and it will be given to you; seek, and you will find; knock, and it will be opened to you."[12]

Start with asking (praying), and you'll receive inner wisdom about what to do. Then go and seek (do) the thing you desire; eventually you'll find it. Finally, when the door stands before you, knock (persevere). The promise is that the door will be opened—in God's will and timing.

Of course, this principle works on many levels. Sometimes all you need do is ask and the answer comes.

1. Ask

George Mueller, the Christian who built orphanages for English children during the nineteenth century, did nothing to raise funds for his projects but ask God for help through prayer. In fact, he never sent a fund-raising letter, never ran a campaign, never even told others of his needs. On one occasion the cupboard was bare, and he had hundreds of children to feed. There was no money and no promise of help from anyone but God. Mueller called all his workers together, and they prayed.

That evening at dinnertime there was a sudden knock on the front door. Mueller answered and found no one, but there on the stoop were bags of wheat, eggs, hams, turkeys, and other items that would feed the whole orphanage for days.

On another occasion shortly before his death, he had more than two thousand children under his care, and almost all the supplies for the orphanage were gone. The food ran out with a hundred youngsters still waiting to be fed. Mueller called all his workers together and again cried, "Pray, brethren, pray!"

That afternoon, over five hundred dollars (in English pounds) was sent to them. Next came a thousand dollars. And only a few days later, over seventy-five hundred dollars came in. It was enough to feed them all for weeks!

During his lifetime, Mueller fed, clothed, and raised more than ninety-five hundred orphans. They didn't go without one meal during his tenure, even though he never told anyone outside the orphanage of their needs. Over seven and a half million dollars were sent in during the sixty years of Mueller's work. In one year alone, over two hundred thousand dollars came in. Yet, they did not have a single committee, fund-raiser, or endowment. It all came in answer to prayer.

In a similar vein, a friend of mine made a mistake during the transition from singleness to marriage.

For the first six months he had no medical insurance. His wife, however, got pregnant shortly after their honeymoon. When he finally did get insurance, the insurer told him the company would not cover anything in the pregnancy or any related complications because it was a "preexisting condition." My friend and his wife embarked upon the last months of the pregnancy with fear in their hearts.

Then the worst happened: The wife began to suffer from toxemia. She was hospitalized and eventually, to save the baby, the doctors performed a cesarean section—all at the young man's cost. His wife was in intensive care for two weeks. The premature baby was in neonatal intensive care for the same period of time. When they left, they were presented with a bill for more than seventeen thousand dollars. As a young minister on a small salary, my friend had no way to pay it. Terribly scared, he prayed for help and also mentioned his plight to the director of his church district.

As he stared at the mountain of bills, he had little hope of paying them except over the course of many years. And more bills were coming in from the anesthesiologists, obstetricians, surgeons, and others involved in the delivery. In a short time, over twenty-four thousand dollars in bills had piled up.

Then God got involved. At first it was a trickle of checks from friends, relatives, and his own church. One hundred dollars here, two hundred dollars there, an occasional three hundred dollars. Then more churches sent gifts. Five-hundred-dollar checks began arriving daily in the mail. At one point, a check for a thousand dollars from an anonymous giver (routed through a local organization) fell out of one of the many envelopes stuffed in his mailbox. In the end, all the immediate bills were paid and a reasonable payment installment program without interest was worked out with the hospital for the rest of the charges.

For my friend, it was an experience of gratitude, joy, and the intense feeling of God's love and commitment to him and his family.

Sometimes all you need do is *ask,* and you will receive. If you believe you can, you can—in the power of Christ.

2. Seek

Often, however, you must go a step beyond asking: You must *seek.* And if you seek, God's promise is that you will find. "Seek and you will find," Jesus said.

William Lloyd Garrison, an abolitionist during those hard days before the outbreak of the Civil War, was so dedicated to dissolving slavery in the United States he started a newspaper in Boston called *The Liberator.* In the first issue, he wrote, "I do not wish to think, or speak, or write, with moderation. . . . I am in earnest. I will not equivocate.

I will not excuse. I will not retreat a single inch. AND I WILL BE HEARD."

Those words soon appeared on the masthead of every issue of *The Liberator.* The newspaper was widely circulated throughout the United States and England. In fact, Garrison was so virulent at times, many antiabolitionists feared the mere mention of their names in his newspaper's columns. Garrison wrote, "If those who deserve the lash feel it and wince at it, I shall be assured I am striking the right persons in the right place."

While many condemned his radical stand on the issue, Garrison was a committed Christian who believed in ending the outrage and gross injustice of human slavery. He supported Abraham Lincoln in the Emancipation Proclamation. When the Civil War was over, Garrison retired. But clearly, he was a man who told himself, "I can because I believe I can in Christ."

Charles Spurgeon, the eloquent nineteenth-century Baptist preacher in London, was once approached by a young man who asked, "How is it that so many are converted through your messages?"

Spurgeon answered, "Tell me this: Do you believe that any one of your sermons should ever convert anyone?"

The man stammered, "Well, no, I'm not so proud as to think I could do that."

"That's the problem. You don't believe it can happen, so it doesn't." The great preacher often instructed his students, "Take a can of kerosene, pour it over your head, and light it. When you stand up to speak, people will come to see you burn." Enthusiasm and fire and confidence go a long way to making your message not only hearable but powerful, he said.

Too often I hear people blame their environment or their upbringing as the reason they were unable to achieve minimal success. Politicians, for instance, are constantly harping on the many "victims" of society, people whose ability to live decent, productive lives is hampered because of how they grew up or what their parents did to them.

In the national best-seller *Awaken the Giant Within*, Anthony Robbins rejects this idea. He tells the story of a cruel drug addict and alcoholic who almost committed suicide several times and is presently serving a life sentence in prison. This man had two sons. One son grew up to be exactly like him, a drug addict and alcoholic who is now serving a prison term for attempted murder. The second son, though, is just the opposite. The father of three children, he loves his wife and enjoys productive work as a regional manager for a major company.

Both young men were asked independently, "Why has your life turned out this way?" Amazingly they both gave a similar answer. "What else could I have become, having grown up with a father like that?"

Robbins goes on to say, "It's not the events of our lives that shape us, but our beliefs as to what those events mean."[13]

It's too easy to say, "Because I was raised in a such-and-such way, I have difficulty living rightly and productively." That's a cop-out. Sure your environment and the difficulties you faced growing up can hinder you. But in many cases they can also help you to choose a better way. The apostle Paul is a primary example. He grew up in a staunchly pharisaic home. He opposed Jesus and all He stood for. He persecuted Christians. Yet he became—because of his beliefs and commitments—the greatest evangelist and apostle in history. Why? Because he believed he could do it in Christ!

3. Knock

In many cases a third step is also required: "Knock, and it will be opened to you." Often you must put legs to your prayers. You must speak, walk, travel, preach, stand and deliver, work, persist—and above all knock and keep knocking till the door falls down.

John Wesley said, "Pray as if it all depended on God, and act as if it all depended on you."

The apostle Paul knew this well. When he and Barnabas were called to plant churches in Asia, they were led by the Holy Spirit, but they had to take action themselves. They had to get from Seleucia to

Cyprus, from Salamis to Paphos, from Paphos to Perga in Pamphylia, and later to Pisidian Antioch. When Paul stood up to preach, certainly the Spirit empowered him; he himself exhorted us all to be "filled with the Spirit." But Paul had to believe—to say, "I can!"—so he would have the courage to confront pagans who had little reason to give up their pleasure-seeking lifestyle.

Paul persevered. He beat a trail throughout Asia, Macedonia, and Italy because he believed intensely that he could do great things for God and the kingdom in the power of Christ.

OTHER AREAS OF LIFE

How does this relate to the sports world or the business world or the political world or the entertainment world?

The principle applies perfectly. Someone gets an idea—an inspiration, a moment of truth—and he forges a plan. He prays about it. He thinks about it. He comes up with variations and options, steps to take and resources to employ; he puts together a blueprint of what he wants to accomplish. Then he sets about doing it. He can because he thinks he can. He does it because he's convinced it will work and succeed. He takes action and succeeds because he's confident God will bring it all to pass.

I told you how, as a twelve-year-old boy, I was

stricken with diabetes mellitus, a major killer of Americans every year. I did not think much about it at the time; I just learned to cope with it. But when I finally decided to go to medical school, I developed a stronger interest in the problem.

I recall well my sophomore year; like everyone else who goes through medical school, I had the sophomore syndrome. My classmates and I would read about tuberculosis and then awaken during the middle of the night in a sweat, thinking, *Oh no! I've contracted TB.* We would read about lymphoma and think, *That lymph node under my arm is a little large. I wonder if I have lymphoma.* We would read about hepatitis and think, *I was around a patient with hepatitis several days ago. My eyes do look a little yellow.* We all became neurotic.

I was handling my neurosis fairly well, I suppose, until I read the following words from our pathology textbook: "All too often the course of diabetes mellitus is a negative one. First, the eyes go, then the kidneys, and then before age thirty, all too often the diabetic dies."

When I read that diabetes was a killer, I immediately went into action. I believed if I didn't, it was all over. There was no point to going on; I'd be dead by thirty. I began meditating on various Scriptures I'd memorized as a disciple with the Navigators. All those great promises came flooding back: "I am with you always," "I will never leave you nor forsake you," "Trust in the LORD with all your heart, / And lean not on your own understanding."[14] I sat up in bed after hours of tossing and turning and resolved, "I can do it in Jesus. I'll make it. I'll get past thirty and forty. I know it can be done."

The next morning I was up at 5:00 A.M. doing push-ups and sit-ups and jogging several miles. I refused to die young; I was ready to fight back physically. I continued fervently memorizing Scripture, reading God's Word, spending time with other Christians, serving in my local church, giving it my all. I wanted to beat the odds!

I later discovered the book was overly negative, but I have never stopped the daily exercise and devotion to God and His Word. Today, in my late forties, I am in better health than I've ever been.

Why? Because I'm better than others? Because I have this idea and it can overcome anything? Because God peered down and commented, "Look at this guy Minirth! We'd better let him live longer, or when he gets up here he'll really be upset"?

Not at all. It has to be because God in His grace supports me, holds me, strengthens me, and walks with me each day. He's a God of great grace!

But what if I didn't do those push-ups every day? What if I just said, "God'll take care of it and I'll just go and eat what I like and not keep physically fit"?

Maybe the Lord would still have grace. Maybe I'd still be alive. But I doubt it. God expects us to take responsibility for our lives. Sure, the blessing must come from Him. Of course He's in charge, and if He decides to take me tomorrow there's nothing I can do to stop it. But at the same time, He expects me to take action, to get into the fight, and to persevere. After all, what did Paul say of himself at the end of his life? "I have fought the good fight, I have finished the race, I have kept the faith."[15]

Was Paul bragging? Was he saying he's better than Peter or me or you? Not at all. He was simply stating the facts: He had not sat back and let go and let God. He'd gotten into the fight and stuck to it.

Does that mean he was saved because of those things? Never! We are saved by God's grace through faith in His Son. There is no work we can do to sufficiently impress God so He'll say, "He's the kind of guy I want in heaven."

But we have a responsibility to act, to obey, to give, to sacrifice, to serve, to love, to worship. Otherwise, what are all those commands in Scripture about? Aren't they the things God wants us to do? Then how are we to do them—by sitting back and hoping for a miracle?

I am convinced God wants us to take action because He intends to work in and through and around us in the process. Jesus told the disciples, "Go therefore and make disciples of all the nations." That's the responsibility part. But He ended the quote with the words, "I am with you always."[16]

That's the grace, the empowering, part. In other words, "You go, and I will work through you. You put this idea into action, and I will bless it."

Another story I've read about George Mueller concerns a trip he made on a ship across the Atlantic to Canada. One day during the passage a heavy fog descended. The ship drifted aimlessly, with its crew unable to get bearings and fearful of running into another ship or even an iceberg. When the situation continued for more than a day, Mueller worked his way amidships and rapped on the captain's door. "I must be in Toronto by Sunday," he informed the captain.

The seaman quickly answered, "In no way can this vessel move without assuming great danger of colliding with another."

Mueller answered, "I understand, but in forty years of Christian service I have not failed to keep an appointment. I must be in Toronto by Sunday!" He invited the captain to attend a special prayer session to entreat God to lift the fog. The captain appeared embarrassed, but he agreed. Together the men knelt and Mueller beseeched the Master. Following suit, more to please Mueller than to pray in genuine faith, the captain intoned a brief petition. But after a moment, Mueller touched his shoulder. "You need not pray," he said. "You do not believe."

The captain was amazed, and they rose to leave

the cabin. As they reached the deck, the two men gazed at the open sea, one in astonishment and the other in a calm "just-as-I-expected" look. The fog had lifted.[17]

Similarly, several years ago, my partner, Dr. Paul Meier, and I considered beginning a radio ministry called "The Minirth Meier New Life Clinic Program." As we looked at the start-up costs, the amount of time needed to produce a daily radio show, and the profound problems of finding the right personnel to run it, I wanted to quit. But the principle—In Christ, I can if I believe I can—bounced back and forth in my mind daily. Again and again Paul and I encouraged one another to think and pray positively, not just because we wanted to succeed—of course we hoped for that—but more because we wanted to minister in the area of psychology and psychiatry, an area some Christians despise.

After we were on the air we fought a lot of battles just to keep the program on some radio stations. In some circumstances we have been canceled with little or no explanation except that the owners simply did not believe in our teaching and ideas, even though we always built them from a scriptural foundation.

What if Paul or I or any of the others had buckled in the crunch and decided the opposition was too formidable, the personal costs too high, the time involvement too wearisome? What if we had just said, "We'll give it a try, but if any pressure comes we'll bail out"? Or what if the apostle Paul had said, "I'll give it a shot, but if it doesn't work after the first try, I'll give up"? What if Gideon or Moses or Abraham or Jesus Himself had murmured into their pillows, "I just don't think it can be done"?

It's not enough to believe God can do it; after all, Scripture tells us God can do anything but sin. We must believe that God can do it *through us*. We must believe He will work in us and through us to bring about the dreams we have in our own hearts.

Ask yourself, "What is my dream?" Is it to own a business? To open a restaurant? To preach the gospel? To run the hundred meters in under nine seconds?

Our dreams and hopes must be tempered by prayer, faith, hope, and above all, realism. Yet we should not be so realistic that we stymie our own efforts.

Charles Kettering, automotive inventor and entrepreneur, said it this way: "A man must have a certain amount of intelligent ignorance to get anywhere." In analyzing a problem, we will usually begin to see the obstacles in our paths. But it's those who don't know it can't be done who often succeed. They don't let their knowledge of the trail's difficulties derail them.

DREAM BIG

If you have a dream, if you want to succeed in a way that advances God's kingdom, helps others, builds your family, and enables you to live abundantly as Christ promised, then tell yourself, "I can through Christ." Such motivators as Norman Vincent Peale have even advocated that we say such words out loud to ourselves over and over.

That's not bad advice. In fact, that's the very idea behind the Old Testament word for *meditation,* which means to murmur or to talk to yourself as you think about an issue or problem or verse of Scripture. David spoke of meditating on God's glory during the watches of the night in Psalm 63:6. In Psalm 145:5 we're exhorted to "meditate on the glorious splendor of [God's] majesty." And Psalm 1 assures us that if we meditate on God's law day and night we'll be happy, productive, secure, and joyous.

David was advising us to take action as we tell ourselves the truths of Scripture. A good start is Philippians 4:13: "I can do all things through Christ who strengthens me." By repeating that to ourselves we ingrain it in our psyches. It turns into a source of motivation and power, not because we're cranking ourselves up into some psychiatric trance or fantasy, but because there is real power in God's Word. He has invested His life into His Word, as Hebrews 4:12 tells us: "The word of God is living and powerful." He has "breathed it out of his mouth," as Paul told Timothy.[18]

By putting those words into our mouths and into

our hearts, we gradually absorb them into the undercurrents of our thinking. Anyone who tells himself or herself repeatedly, "I can through Christ" will eventually believe it and begin to act upon it.

Solomon wrote in Proverbs 23:7, "as [a man] thinks in his heart, so is he." He meant that what you think is what you really are. If you believe you can accomplish some task, pursue some dream, start some enterprise, or win some contest, chances are you will if you believe with all your heart that you can—through prayer, hard work, all-out effort, and the support of Jesus Christ.

Marie Curie, the codiscoverer of radium, was one of the world's great scientists. Twice a winner of the Nobel Prize (in 1903 for physics and in 1911 for chemistry), she knew both the power of personal confidence and the hard work it takes to succeed. She once said, "Life is not easy for any of us. But what of that? We must have perseverance and, above all, confidence in ourselves. We must believe that we are gifted for something, and that this thing, at whatever cost, must be attained."

CONFIDENCE IN OURSELVES

Again, I have to ask myself, is confidence in myself a repudiation of basic biblical teaching? No, for isn't that exactly what is required to accomplish anything—from riding your first bike to designing a nuclear submarine to persuading a friend to consider the claims of Christ? Isn't that precisely what Jesus instructed His disciples to do as they went into all the world to reclaim it for Christ? Didn't Peter have to walk out of the Upper Room and start speaking? Didn't Jesus Himself have to set His face like flint and head off for Jerusalem and the cross? Don't such actions require confidence—the sense in your own heart that your cause is right, your Lord is with you, your skills are in place, and all you have to do is step up to the ticket counter? It's not an act of pride. It's not vanity. It's not even ego. It's your basic, meat-and-potatoes, charcoal-grilled faith.

Faith produces confidence that says, "I can through Christ." The Lord longs to hear these words: "Jesus, I'm really going to take You at Your word. I'm going to rely on it completely. I'm going to stick my neck out. I'm going to lay it all on the line. If this fails, I'm done for, so I'm depending completely on You to work it out. I'll take care of the details and the legwork. But You have to come through, Lord, or it'll crash."

I honestly think the Lord loves that kind of faith/confidence/belief commitment. Don't you?

Any person anywhere can formulate a plan and choose a course of action and go at it hammer and tongs. If he or she believes it can be done, nothing will stop that person. Not people. Not problems. Not obstacles so big the sun itself is obscured.

Nothing—except perhaps one Person: God Himself. If God chooses to say no, then of course he or she cannot succeed.

But that's the kicker. For the Christian living in intimacy, love, and commitment to Christ, there is no NO. "If you abide in Me, and My words abide in you, you will ask what you desire, and it shall be done for you."[19]

Solomon coined it well: "Commit your works to the LORD, / And your thoughts will be established."[20]

A FEW QUALIFICATIONS

Before we leave this chapter several qualifications should be made regarding the principle, In Christ, you can if you believe you can:

1. While the principle is definitely powerful and can be of great benefit, it certainly has limitations. People have had great guilt because they thought they could get over cancer and did not. The brain does try to respond physiologically to what we ask, but there are limits to what it can do.

2. While the principle is powerful and can be of great benefit, it can be used for the wrong purpose. A man can believe he can accomplish great material wealth—and he may, but only to realize later he made the wrong investment and lost his family and other real values in life.

3. While the principle is powerful and can be of

great benefit, it is not nearly as powerful as God Himself. Only God could part the Red Sea, bring the plagues on Egypt, bring down the walls of Jericho, or convert Paul.

4. While the principle is powerful and can be of great benefit, God may actually oppose it at times. This was shown in Genesis 11:6: "And the LORD said, 'Indeed the people are one and they all have one language, and this is what they begin to do; now nothing that they propose to do will be withheld from them.'" God did stop the builders of the Tower of Babel with their self-centered "I-can" attitude.

5. With these cautions in mind, the principle is powerful and can be of great benefit if one uses it for the glory of Christ: I can through Christ.

I am convinced that most individuals limit themselves; it's not God who limits them. They could do so much more if only they believed they could. All the power of our bodies' physiology, our minds, and our faith are at our disposal. The power is our choice. "I can, through Christ" is the first principle for beating the odds. If you believe you can succeed at your dream, you most assuredly will succeed—in Christ, through Christ, and for Christ.

Jan Paderewski, the renowned pianist and the prime minister of Poland in 1919, was once asked if he could perform a recital on short notice. Paderewski is said to have replied, "I'm always ready. I have practiced eight hours daily for forty years."

The man who asked him, also a pianist, said, "I wish I had been born with such determination."

Paderewski answered, "We are all born with it. I just used mine."

He could because he believed he could.

CHAPTER 3

The Triangle of Power

2 *Support Your Life with the Bible, Prayer, and the Church*

Military people, architects, and designers know that one of the most secure devices to build strength into a structure is the triangle. Tripods are the easiest way to hold up objects with the least amount of effort.

It's with that idea in mind that I speak of the "triangle of strength." Where does the strength of God come from? How do we tap into His power and allow it to transform our lives? I see three points of the triangle necessary for beating the odds: the Word of God, prayer, and the church. Let's look at these individually to get a grasp of what they really mean.

THE FIRST SIDE OF THE TRIANGLE OF POWER: THE BIBLE

The Bible is God's Word, His unchanging message for a changing world. 1 John 2:14 says that the young men "are strong, and the word of God abides in [them], and [they] have overcome the wicked one." John is saying that the Word is powerful enough to overcome the world and the devil.

And the Word is so powerful it created our universe: "By faith we understand that the worlds were framed by the word of God, so that the things which are seen were not made of things which are visible."[1] I have thought about what this verse says about the universe. God spoke His word and formed all the worlds, galaxies, planets, suns, and moons. Everything in the heavens came into being at a word from God. How big is the Milky Way? Traveling at 186,000 miles per second, the speed of light, how long would it take to cross the Milky Way in a spaceship? One hundred thousand years! And the Milky Way is only one of billions and billions of known galaxies.

I thought about that and realized that if God formed all those worlds with a word, how powerful His living Word—our Bibles—must be! The more of God's Word we get into our lives, the more power we will discover.

But that's all theory. Just how powerful is this Word of God?

SOME WITNESSES

Martin Luther said, "The Bible is alive, it speaks to me; it has feet, it runs after me; it has hands, it lays hold on me." Timothy Dwight worded it this way: "The Bible is a window in this prison-world, through which we may look into eternity." And Billy Graham coined this idea about it: "The Bible is the constitution of Christianity."

Just how powerful is the Bible to convict and convert men and women? The apostle Paul, one of the greatest evangelists of all time, told the Hebrew Christians, "The word of God is living and powerful, and sharper than any two-edged sword, piercing even to the division of soul and spirit, and of joints and marrow."[2] God's Word has innate power. It pierces people to the very roots of their being and exposes the truth in ways that no human word can. This was true in Paul's time, and it's true today. Its power extends throughout settings as unlikely as the Acropolis of ancient Greece—and even the theaters of modern Russia.

While Russia was still a communist country, a Russian matinée idol named Alexander Rostovzev played the role of Jesus in a blasphemous communist play, *Christ in a Tuxedo*. The script called for him to read two verses from the Sermon on the Mount and then to cry, "Give me my tuxedo and top hat!" But as he read from the biblical text, "Blessed are the poor in spirit, for theirs is the kingdom of heaven. Blessed are those who mourn, for they shall be comforted," he had no further power to say the words of the script. Instead, he began to tremble. He attempted to speak his next lines several times. Finally he began reading from the rest of Matthew 5. He ignored the stamping feet and coughs of the actors around him. He couldn't stop! Then, remembering a line from his childhood in the Russian Orthodox Church, he suddenly shouted, "Lord, remember me when Thou comest into Thy kingdom." He went backstage, and before the curtain was lowered, he had committed his life to Christ.[3]

In another case, an Indian poet named Tilak was traveling on a train in Europe. An Englishman befriended him while the other Europeans snubbed the dark-skinned Indian. After some time in conversation, the Englishman gave Tilak a New Testament, urging him to read it. "If you study it, you will be a Christian within two years." Tilak smiled, thinking this was quite impossible.

However, the friendship and courtesy of the man led Tilak to begin reading the New Testament, and it was not long before he accepted Jesus. He later testified, "I could not tear myself away from its burning words of truth."[4]

Sergei Kourdakov, at one time a member of Russia's secret police, a force developed to persecute and stamp out Christians, wrote a book called *The Persecutor* about his own confrontation with the Lord of the Word even as he tried to destroy the faith in his homeland. He had his first chance to read and study the words of Jesus because of a lovely young Christian woman named Natasha whom he admired.

He wrote, "That night, at the first opportunity I had, lying in my bunk at the Naval Academy, I opened up those pieces of paper and began to read them again. Jesus was talking and teaching someone how to pray. I became more curious and read on. This certainly was no antistate material. It was how to be a better person and how to forgive those who do you wrong. Suddenly the words leaped out of those pages and into my heart. I read on, engrossed in the kind words of Jesus. This was exactly the opposite of what I had expected. My lack of understanding, which had been like blinders on my eyes, left me right then, and the words bit deeply into my being. It was as though somebody were in the room with me, teaching me those words and what they said. They made a profound impact on me. I read them again and again, then sat thinking, my mind lost in the wonder of it all. *So this is what Natasha believed.*

"The words grabbed my heart. I was somehow

frightened and uneasy, like a man walking on unfamiliar ground. I read the words and reread them and put them down, and still they came back to my mind again and again. Those words were leading Natasha to be a better person and help others. They haunted me. It was a feeling totally new to me."[5]

Kourdakov's words attest plainly and powerfully to the innate might of the Word of God. But that is only the power of God's Word to convict and save. What of its power to transform?

THE BIBLE'S POWER TO TRANSFORM YOU AND ME

Time and time again I have meditated on a truth until it became part of me, and slowly I have seen difficulties with anger, prejudice, hatred, and insensitivity melt away. One of the greatest stories of God's power to transform through His Word is found in the classic novel *The Mutiny on the Bounty*. When Fletcher Christian and his fellow mutineers put Captain Bligh and those loyal to him adrift in a little boat, Christian and his men knew they had to escape. Nine of the sailors then sailed with Christian to a South Sea island—Pitcairn Island—and set up homes with some native women. They lived a debauched life, learning to make whiskey from a plant found on the island, and this led to their ruin. Diseases common to that part of the world struck. Several died from internecine warfare. There was killing and immorality.

Eventually, all the white men and native men were dead except one white man, Alexander Smith. Among the possessions of one of the dead sailors, Smith found a Bible and began studying it for himself, partly in his loneliness and partly as a means to find a way out of the pit they had all dug for themselves. The book was completely new to him; he'd never seen a Bible or read it. Gradually, God's words had a powerful effect on him, and he began applying them in his life and teaching them to the women and children who were still alive.

Twenty years later, when the first ship dropped anchor in their little harbor, the newcomers found the people living in genuine harmony, with compassion, goodness, kindness, and love—no crime, disease, immorality, illiteracy, insanity, or lack of faith. Why? Because Smith and his people had taken God's Word to heart, and it had transformed them.

Abraham Lincoln said, "I believe the Bible is the best gift that God has ever given to man. All the good from the Savior of the world is communicated to us through this book. I have been driven many times to my knees by the overwhelming conviction that I had nowhere else to go."

How do we achieve such an intimate relationship with God's Word? I believe six steps are necessary before we can really hear God's voice:

1. Read the Bible again and again.

Read it straight through. Spend fifteen minutes a day in the Word, just reading it; this will allow you to cover both testaments in a year.

Ask yourself "What if . . . ?" What if I take it upon myself to attempt what Paul did in missions? Will God be with me? What if I face this problem as Jesus counseled, with faith and prayer? Can I overcome it in His power? What if I let the Bible lead me and I apply this truth to the terrible situations I'm facing in my marriage? Can it grant me victory?

Anthony Robbins, author of *Awaken the Giant Within,* said questions are the crucial first steps to becoming all you were meant to be—and, I add, in Christ. He wrote, "Questions set off a processional effect that has an impact beyond our imagination. Questioning our limitations is what tears down the walls in life—in business, in relationships, between countries. I believe all human progress is preceded by new questions."[6]

He went on to give an example from his own life. He returned from a business trip and found that his partner had embezzled a quarter of a million dollars and run up a company debt of three-quarters of a million. He was almost devastated. But he asked himself a question: *How can I turn this around?* He even pushed it further, asking, *How can I turn my company around, take it to the next level, and cause it to have even more impact than it ever has in the past?*

That moved his company from disaster to triumph. Eventually more than seven million of his tapes were distributed worldwide. Why? Because Robbins asked the right question.

I don't know what Anthony Robbins thinks of Jesus or the Bible, but I do know he propounds a rich principle. Read the Bible and ask yourself the great questions—"What if?" and "Why not?" and "What about me?" and you will find yourself moving forward rather than standing still or even losing ground.

2. Meditate on God's words.

Psalm 119:11 says, "Your word I have hidden in my heart, / That I might not sin against You." And verse 9, "How can a young man cleanse his way? By taking heed according to Your word." The Scriptures tell us repeatedly to meditate on it, think the words through, and turn them over and over in our hearts until they are embedded there like letters chiseled in stone.

3. Ask God to make His words real in your life.

Turn the words of Scripture into your own prayers. People ask, "How do I pray according to the will of God?" How? Simply turn Scripture into your prayer!

Each year I find a verse that I meditate on and

think about as my "year's verse." Recently my verse was 1 Chronicles 4:10. Here, Jabez prays, "Oh, that You would bless me indeed, and enlarge my territory, that Your hand would be with me, and that You would keep me from evil, that I may not cause pain." Following those words, the writer says, "So God granted him what he requested."

What a verse to meditate on and pray through! I have done that and seen God "bless me indeed," and "enlarge my territory" through an expanding ministry on the radio and in print. He has "kept me from evil" too. Every time we thought the clinic was going to be destroyed, God turned the situation to good, according to His promise in Romans 8:28: "And we know that all things work together for good to those who love God, to those who are the called according to His purpose."

One such instance occurred about seven years ago when Paul Meier and I cosigned a note with a real estate investor on several buildings in Texas, one of which was right down the street from our main offices in Richardson. At the time this building seemed to be a major burden. With the devaluation of real estate properties, we could not sell it for the amount we owed on it. So we thought of creative ways we could utilize the space.

We finally decided to convert the building into a day hospital where patients could receive daily counseling much like that offered in a hospital setting and then return to their homes at night. A few years later the insurance companies changed their qualification standards for hospitalization treatment drastically. Now an insurance company will not cover inpatient hospitalization unless a patient is psychotic or imminently suicidal. I believe God turned a potentially damaging situation into a blessing for us; before we ever foresaw this change we established this continuum of care where people can have inpatient, day hospital, or outpatient care. If we're creative and listen to God's direction, it's hard to stamp us out.

4. Apply the Scriptures to your problems.

If you are struggling in a certain area of life, go to a concordance and look up a key word such as *worry*. Find the verses that talk about worry, then memorize them, pray through them, and apply them. Make them live in your life. Become a walking, living, breathing illustration of what the Bible says.

D. L. Moody said, "God did not give us the Scriptures to increase our knowledge, but to change our lives." Through the Word of God, Christ gives us that abundant life He promised in John 10:10.

5. Share the Word with others.

When the opportunity is right, tell others what God is doing in your life. You have seen Him work in your life because you've done all these things. Now tell the world. As David said in Psalm 145:11–12, "They shall speak of the glory of Your kingdom, / And talk of Your power, / To make known to the sons of men His mighty acts, / And the glorious majesty of His kingdom."

6. Never stop learning, studying, and growing in the Word.

Peter tells us at the end of his second letter, "But grow in the grace and knowledge of our Lord and Savior Jesus Christ."[7] How do you grow? By ingesting and feeding on God's Word for as long as you live. Memorizing Scripture has been my number-one habit ever since I joined the Navigators. I can honestly testify it's the one thing that has had a greater impact on my life than anything else.

James M. Boice tells the story of Dr. Emile Cailliet, a French philosopher who was brought up with a secular education and no interest in spiritual things. As he fought in the trenches during World War I he thought of Levin, in Leo Tolstoy's *Anna Karenina,* who asked the great questions: Where does life come from? What does it all mean? What does science or any other source of human wisdom give us in the face of death and eternity? Cailliet had no answers, and like Levin he said, "I too felt, not with my reason but with my whole being, that I was destined to perish miserably when the hour came."

As Cailliet stood guard duty one night, he determined to write a book that would answer these questions. He secretly began collecting quotes and thoughts of great men as well as his own thoughts into a book he carried with him. Even when he was wounded and released, he continued. Finally, he felt he had finished the book, so he sat down under a tree and opened to the first page. As he read, a great depression rolled over him as he realized the words were all fabrications of human wisdom. He put the book back into his pocket, dejected and miserable.

Amazingly, at that moment, his wife arrived home and told him she'd gotten a Bible from a local Huguenot pastor. She didn't even know why she'd gone to the little chapel, and she was a bit afraid of what her husband would think, knowing he was so against religion.

Immediately, Cailliet took the Bible and began reading. He would later write, "I opened and 'chanced' upon the Beatitudes! I read, and read, and read—now aloud with an indescribable warmth surging within. . . . I could not find words to express my own awe and wonder. And suddenly the realization dawned upon me: This was the Book that would understand me! . . .

"The Providential circumstances amid which the Book had found me now made it clear that while it seemed absurd to speak of a book understanding a man, this could be said of the Bible because its pages were animated by the Presence of the Living God and the Power of His mighty acts. To this God I prayed that night, and the God who answered was the same God of whom it was spoken in the Book."[8]

Cailliet settled in America and taught at Princeton Theological Seminary as a professor of that Book!

God's Word is powerful. Take it, feed on it, love it, and make it your own.

The Bible is the first side of the triangle of power. In the Word we hear God's voice—encouraging, challenging, convicting, guiding us in all circumstances. In prayer, the second side of the triangle, we respond to God with praise, love, adoration, requests, and supplications for others.

THE SECOND SIDE OF THE TRIANGLE OF POWER: PRAYER

What is prayer? Cameron Thompson, in his book, *Master Secrets of Prayer,* defined it this way: "Prayer is the breathing and panting of the spirit after God. It is taking hold of the willingness of God, rather than an overcoming of His reluctance. It is a tuning in on the great, thunderous two-thousand-year-old prayer meeting going on in the glory above."

It astonishes me: The Creator God bids you and me to come into His throne room and lay down our entreaties. Not even the president has done that with you or me, and yet the living God says we can do it every moment of every day!

Receiving a word from God in the Bible moves us to respond to Him. If it's a promise from God, we might respond with thanks and praise and the desire to make that promise happen in our lives. If it's a word of warning, we take it to heart and assure the Lord that we honestly want to avoid the sin He has pointed out. If it's a word of insight, we mull over it, ask questions of the Spirit of God, and await His answers. God's Word is God talking to us. Prayer is our responding to God. Both are paramount.

Martin Luther once said, "I have so much to do that I must spend the first three hours of each day in prayer." Considering that Luther is the most written about personality in history besides Jesus Christ, you would think prayer would have taken a backseat to all his other chores. That was not his way, or the way with any serving, striving Christian.

John Wesley, founder of the Methodist faith, made this boast: "Give me one hundred preachers who fear nothing but sin, and desire nothing but God, and I care not a straw whether they be clergymen or laymen; such alone will shake the gates of hell and set up the kingdom of heaven on earth. God does nothing but in answer to prayer."[9]

Even Albert Einstein, the great scientist, wondered about the importance of prayer. In 1952 a doctoral student at Princeton asked him, "What is there left in the world for original dissertation research?" Einstein, a visiting lecturer, said, "Find out about prayer. Somebody must find out about prayer."

Plenty of somebodies have—all through history. Jenny Lind, famed opera singer of the nineteenth century who was called the "Swedish Nightingale," always prayed before each performance, which was said to be a marvel of vocal intensity and beauty. Her maid told her biographers that she would then strike one clear, vibrant note and hold it for as long as she was able. Finally, she would pray, "Master, let me ring true tonight. Let me ring true, as Thou art true."

George Mueller, some of whose stories I have already recounted, spoke of living in the aura and spirit of prayer. Asked about his pattern and habit of prayer and how long he prayed each day, he said, "Hours every day. I live in the spirit of prayer; I pray as I walk, when I lie down and when I rise and the answers are always coming."

David Brainerd, whose famed diary has been passed on to whole generations of believers, struggled in the early 1700s to reach the New England Indian tribes with the message of Christ. So great was his commitment and fervor that he spent whole days in prayer, beseeching God and sweating intensely even though he was lying in the snow. He could not even speak the language of the people; to speak his message to the people he had to rely on an interpreter who was so drunk he could hardly stand up. Yet some of his early sermons were so overwhelming that scores of Indians trusted Christ and became committed believers.

Such words and stories encourage me to stay in that spirit of prayer every day. I find myself praying before a broadcast; before, during, and after appointments; in restaurants; while waiting in line at the grocery store—*everywhere*. Every free moment becomes a moment to come before God's throne and talk to Him about what I'm thinking and feeling. God wants us to be His closest friends. He wants us to come into an intimate fellowship with Him that leads us to tell Him everything that is in our hearts, whether it's a psalm of love or a bitter lament. Take a look at the mountain you have to climb and then invite Him to come along and even guide you to the top.

God never fails to answer an honest, forthright, specific prayer. He may say, "No." He may say, "Yes." He may say, "Wait" or "Maybe." Tryon Edwards said, "Never think that God's delays are God's denials. True prayer always receives what it asks, or something better."

Jerry Hopkins is quoted in *Decision* magazine as saying, "Prayer could bring about a religious revival in our nation that would literally sweep the world. Prayer can change a cold, lifeless, self-centered church into a powerhouse where hundreds could be won to Christ. And here is one place where many of us have utterly failed. We place much emphasis on man power, the power of organization, the power of money and finances, the power of drives and promotion; but we are still in the dark because we have failed to look to the power of prayer—a power that gets for us what God can do."

I'm convinced we haven't seen even the tip of the iceberg of what God can do with people who pray daily, fervently, expectantly. Knowing God works in response to our prayers, we can change history. I don't mean change history in the sense that we can tamper with His eternal plan, but no one knows what that is until it happens. And the marvel is that God invites us to try to change His mind about something we're disturbed or concerned about; He invites us to move Him to action simply by making a simple request.

Some of God's most remarkable answers to prayer are found in Dick Eastman's little book on prayer, *No Easy Road.* In it he relates many stories of Rees Howells, a missionary to Africa. As Howells and several other missionaries were preparing to leave for Africa they realized quite suddenly they'd all forgotten to bring watches, raincoats, or fountain pens. They hadn't told anyone about their need.

Just before their ship left port a friend walked up to them and asked, "What kind of watches do you

have? My son wants to supply you with watches."
Dumbfounded, the missionaries gratefully told
him they had none.

Then the man asked, "Have you prepared for the
rainy seasons in Africa by getting raincoats?"

Again Howells replied they hadn't, so the man
wrote down an address where they could get raincoats at his expense. Finally, as the man wrote, he
looked up and said, "Have you seen this kind of
fountain pen?"

"No," Howells said, his eyes growing wide with
wonder. Immediately, the man gave each of them
one.[10]

It always astonishes me to read such stories.
Something in us wants to dispute such evidence, as
if God really wouldn't do such things. But why not?
I have seen God answer small prayers many times.

As a friend of mine was making his daily hike
around the neighborhood, praying and meditating
on Scripture, he stopped at a local fast-food restaurant for lunch. Dawdling, he suddenly realized he
would be late for an appointment unless he could
get a ride back home. But he didn't see anyone he
knew. He was about to walk out when someone
popped up and asked him, "Are you so-and-so?"
naming him.

"Yes," he answered.

The man said, "I read one of your articles recently
and just wanted to thank you for it. It was great."

He then offered my friend a ride home, right out of the blue.

Why do these things happen? Because we have a God who loves us and answers even our smallest needs.

In his commentary on Philippians, James M. Boice tells another remarkable story of how a man named Hotchkiss, a missionary to Nigeria for more than forty years, was miraculously saved one afternoon. He had received a pith helmet in the mail and was so busy showing it off that he became late for a service in a village located on the other side of a large plain. In those days the rule in Nigeria was never to cross an open space like that on foot for fear of stampedes by wild animals. There was always a safer path along the tree line. But Hotchkiss was late, and he decided to chance it. Halfway across this open area a herd of rhinoceroses thundered down upon him. There was nowhere he could run, so he simply sank down on his knees and began praying, awaiting his meeting with the Savior. The roar around him grew louder and louder until it seemed to envelop him. Then it faded into the distance. Hotchkiss opened his eyes. He arose and stood in the middle of the plain, surrounded by large rhinoceros hoofprints all around him.

Years later, friends from Ohio visited Hotchkiss in Africa. As they met and talked happily, the husband suddenly said, "You know, I had a most unusual experience once that concerned you. . . . One night I woke up suddenly with an irresistible urge to pray for you. And I did, committing you to God's safekeeping."

"Do you remember when it was?" Hotchkiss asked.

"Yes," answered the husband. "I wrote it down that night in my Bible." His summons to prayer had occurred the same day and hour that Hotchkiss had been on that plain.[11]

How can we explain such things, except that we have a great God who answers prayer? And how can each of us experience such answers? Several principles have been important to me:

1. Pray without ceasing as you go about your day.

Learn to live in the flow of prayer. As Paul said in 1 Thessalonians 5:17, "Pray without ceasing."

2. Keep a notebook of your prayers so you can record answers as they occur.

Some people use a journal. This is a good idea because it will be your own memorial book of God's work in your life.

3. Offer to pray for others, and solicit their prayers for yourself.

Don't be proud. Of course you should choose your prayer partners carefully, seeking people you know will follow through. Offer to pray for others, and ask them to pray for you—in church, at work, in the home.

4. Use the Scriptures to guide your prayers.

If you don't know what to pray for or what God's will is on an issue, go to the Bible. Turn its words into your prayers.

5. Learn to pray the moment someone gives you a request.

Because people are constantly soliciting my prayers, it's hard to remember all those requests, or even write them down. So I often simply pray the moment the request is made or the first chance I get after a conversation.

6. When you don't know what to ask, ask the Spirit to ask!

Remember Romans 8:26, "The Spirit Himself makes intercession for us with groanings which cannot be uttered." Sometimes our pain is so great we don't know what to ask. But the Spirit knows. Let Him guide you if you're not sure what to say.

8. Be specific.

Don't be vague or too general. Sure, God can "bless Africa," or "help the missionaries in Europe." But it's better to be as specific as you can so you know when God has answered.

9. Don't give up.

In Luke 18:1 we find these words: "Then He spoke a parable to them, that men always ought to pray and not lose heart." Jesus went on to tell the parable of the unjust judge who only responded to people when they nearly knocked down his door. Jesus makes the point that if an unjust judge responds to a man coming repeatedly for legal protection, how much more will God, who is good, loving, and perfect, respond speedily to us?

The Word and prayer are the first two legs of the triangle of power. The third is the church.

THE THIRD SIDE OF THE TRIANGLE OF POWER: THE CHURCH

It is God's people—the church—who will change the world. It is God's church that will support us and love us and be close to us when we hurt and suffer. It is the people in the pew who hug us when we're down, encourage us when we want to give up, and cheer us on as we serve God with courage and hope. If the Word is God talking to us and prayer is our talking to God, then the church is God's way of walking and living among us. "Two are better than one," says Ecclesiastes 4:9–10, "because they have a good reward for their labor. For if they fall, one will lift up his companion. But woe to him who is alone when he falls, for he has no one to help him up."

We need the wisdom, counsel, friendship, and support of people in our churches. We're like the kid who was afraid during a thunderstorm. His dad told him God was with him. "Yes, I know," he replied. "But I need someone with skin on." I find that I can barely live a day without conferring with close friends in the church or in our ministry or in our clinic. I need their thoughts and advice for many things you might think I would work out myself. As Solomon said in Proverbs 24:6, "In a multitude of counselors there is safety."

The vast majority of people I see in the hospital, many of whom are suffering from depression, do not feel they have one friend in the world. That's not necessarily an accurate reflection of them; instead, it's a picture of America today. In our mobile culture we're afraid to get close to people because we know one of us may soon be moving to another place. We're also fearful of letting others know who we really are because they might not like what they see.

In the battle to beat the odds, undoubtedly the greatest factor that can destroy a person is the sense of isolation, of being alone against the world. In the counseling office many people voice this difficulty: "I just feel so alone." "I wish I didn't feel so isolated about this." "If I only knew there was someone who really supported me." The feeling that you are alone can destroy your morale, hope, ambition, and even your will to live.

During World War II the Nazis conducted studies about how to break a man in prison. They discovered that the surest way was solitary confinement. A few days alone in the dark and cold and a man was ready to tell anything they wanted to know. Few can stand the absolute dark and sense of lostness in that kind of desolation.

In the same way, Satan loves to get Christians alone, in spiritual darkness, or just away on a trip in a lonely hotel. Men and women who seemed strong and unbending with their families and in their churches have given in to awful sins when they were alone with their temptations.

So what is the church? Is it all the good guys, the decent people, the cream of the crop? Not at all. Paul said in 1 Corinthians 1:27–30 that God chose the foolish, weak, base, and despised in order to shame the world. In 1 Corinthians 6:9–11, Paul said the church was composed of people who had been fornicators, idolaters, adulterers, effeminate, homosexuals, thieves, covetous, drunkards, revilers, and swindlers.

On one occasion, Dr. Ray Stedman who founded and pastored Peninsula Bible Church in Palo Alto, California, read this very passage in his church and asked if there were any people present who had any of those sins in their background. That day a man who had been an inveterate and hardened gambler was present; he had converted only two weeks before and was very nervous about being in church.

After Stedman read 1 Corinthians 6:9–10 and asked people to stand, this man looked about the church to see what would happen. The first person who got up was a little old lady in the pew right in front of the gambler! People gasped. Then others stood and soon nearly two-thirds of the people in the sanctuary were on their feet to testify to God's power to transform sinners. The gambler was astonished; he said to himself as he rose to his feet, *Now these are my kind of people!*

That's the church. Sinners. Lost people come to Christ. People who have been changed under the guiding light and presence of Jesus in their lives.

E. Stanley Jones, the well-known missionary to India, once spoke of a young Burmese man who came to the missionaries' ashram in search of fellowship. As he went away, he said, "I came here a flickering torch, but I go away a flaming torch." This happened every time people came to their churches, Jones said.

It's true. A lone coal will not burn nearly so brightly as many coals together, and a lone coal is always in danger of going out.

FRIENDS IN THE CHURCH

When facing insurmountable odds, the first thing a Christian should do is seek the advice, help, love, comfort, and friendship of God's people. Remember how Peter was released from prison in Acts 12? As the people were praying for his release an angel opened the door and he walked out. Then when he arrived at the house where the people were praying, everyone was surprised! In fact, the servant girl who answered the door was so astounded she forgot to open the door; when she announced to the people Peter was out there, they thought it was a ghost!

That's God's people! We pray for a miracle, and when it happens we don't believe it!

It's essential that every Christian build close friendships in his or her church and between churches. How many times have you been bolstered by the counsel and comfort of a good Christian friend? Often, the objective insight of a Christian brother or sister is just what is needed to help us face and win against the odds.

Our Daily Bread carried a story of a pastor who attended a Texas convention of many Mexican

Christians. While there he received news that his wife had been stricken with an illness, and he left for home. On the train back, he spent a sleepless, depressed night, full of anxiety about his wife. The next morning the conductor gave him a telegram, relayed by the previous station. He was sure it contained more disheartening news.

As he read, tears filled his eyes. It was not from home, but from the Christians he'd left at the convention. It said, "Mexican convention in session all night. Prayed for you and your wife. She will get well!"

When he arrived home he found his wife alive and recovering.

That is fellowship. That is friendship, loving, supporting, enduring friendship. Humorist Elbert Hubbard said, "Your friend is the man who knows all about you, and still likes you." I have a number of such friends in my life, and I am grateful for them.

Ralph Waldo Emerson, the American philosopher and transcendentalist, wrote, "The glory of friendship is not the outstretched hand, nor the kindly smile nor the joy of companionship; it is the spiritual inspiration that comes to one when he discovers that someone else believes in him and is willing to trust him."

And C. S. Lewis, a favorite writer of many Christians, said, "Friendship is born at that moment when one person says to another, 'What! You, too? I thought I was the only one.'"

That's the kind of friendship the church creates. Here's how you can make it happen for you:

1. Go to church.

Select one that fits your particular beliefs and model, though I would say you should pick one that preaches and believes the Bible as God's Word. Serve. Give. Share. Get to know people.

2. Begin to develop relationships, first with groups and then with couples and individuals.

Confide your deeper needs, thoughts, and feelings to a few you feel you can trust. Don't hold back. Laugh a little; in fact, laugh a lot. Play games. Have family outings together. Maybe share a sport or an interest in a hobby. Just talk. Show that you rely on certain people for advice and help by going to them for advice and help.

Confess your sins to your close friends. Offer to pray for them, and give them your prayer requests. Be accountable to others for how you're living as a Christian.

3. Build relationships that include accountability, prayer, and commitment.

Unfortunately, churches today seem to lack accountability. In too many churches no one does anything about a problematic person until it's too late; no one wants to get involved. This must stop. We need one another and must reach out in light of that need.

REAL POWER

There is power in this triangle of strength. Through the Word of God, prayer, and fellowship, any one of us can stand firm and beat the odds every time. Yet without each component, the triangle falls. A two-legged stool will never stand. Yet a three-legged stool becomes a rock holding us close to the Lord so He can lead us effectively against any storm where the odds look overwhelming, even impossible.

Name anyone who faced insurmountable odds in the Bible, and if he or she triumphed it was because that person believed God's Word and acted on it. Think of Gideon. He was the least member of his family, his family was the least family of the tribe, and the tribe was the least tribe in Israel. When God was ready to beat the odds, He chose the least of the least of the least. I've come to see that God likes those kinds of odds.

God chose Gideon, a man beating out the last of his wheat in a winepress, to lead His army against the Midianites. This man would repeatedly test God because of a lack of faith and a fear of the Midianites, a nation of wealthy nomads who had overcome the Israelites and ruled over them, raiding their villages and trampling their crops. Gideon tested God with his well-known fleeces. First, he told God, "I shall put a fleece of wool on the threshing floor; if there is dew on the fleece only, and it is dry on all the ground, then I shall know that You will save Israel by my hand."[12] The next day, only the fleece was wet, but still Gideon questioned. He asked God to reverse the sign. And the next day, the ground was wet and the fleece was dry. God's answer was obvious.

Despite all Gideon's fear and anxiety God chose him and then chose only three hundred men to go with him. Initially, there were three hundred thousand men. But the odds were too high: five Israelites to two Midianites. Then God cut the number of men to ten thousand, making the odds twelve to one. Still too great for God! So God cut the number of men to three hundred. The odds were now four hundred to one against Gideon and his little band of men—just God's kind of odds. God's Word gives us the power to beat the odds no matter how great they may be!

CHAPTER 4

The Total Person

 Take Care of All of You

The great baseball pitcher Satchel Paige was renowned for his "Paige-isms," his often witty but sobering ways of dispensing truth. Some of Paige's best known bits of advice are:

- "Avoid fried meats that angry up the blood."
- "If your stomach disputes you, lie down and pacify it with cool thoughts."
- "Keep the juices flowing by jangling around gently as you move."
- "Go light, very light, on the vices, such as carrying around in society. The society rumble ain't restful."
- "Avoid running at all times."
- "Don't look back. Something might be gaining on you."[1]

Not bad advice, and good for producing a little laughter. All humor aside, though, maintaining your physical, mental, and spiritual health is a key to overcoming the odds in your life. Without health in all three areas, we are destined for failure.

Certainly, there are times when physical and even mental health is impossible. Illness is unavoidable at times. Researchers are finding that mental health is more closely connected to biological rhythms and factors than ever before. An internal chemical glitch can produce a harrowing depression even when a person seemed to be in excellent health.

On the other hand, in our world today we have tremendous control over our own health. In fact, lack of spiritual, mental, or physical health is far more often a result of negligence and/or abuse than anything else. Alcoholism, smoking, drug addiction, promiscuity, violence, and numerous other plain old sins contribute to ill health and premature death far more than cancer or heart disease or any other five other biological killers (cancer, heart disease, tuberculosis, malaria, multiple sclerosis, etc.) combined.

Athletes know their performance on the playing field is always contingent on how they spend their time and effort off the field. In one of the *Rocky* movies, Rocky's trainer tells him that for every minute in the ring a boxer has to train a thousand minutes in private. It's really the same for us. For every minute we struggle with a stack of troubles, we'll probably spend many hours in normal living, free of difficulties. In those times we must develop the habits and patterns that ensure we can defeat the enemy when he attacks.

Thus, my third principle concerns taking care of ourselves. If we don't take care of ourselves, who will? As the slogan of the American Health Foundation goes, "Nobody takes better care of you than you."

God does not free us from responsibility when we sinfully abuse our bodies, minds, or spirits. The apostle Paul told the Colossians, "He who does wrong will be repaid for the wrong which he has done, and there is no partiality."[2] He warned the Galatians, "Do not be deceived, God is not mocked; for whatever a man sows, that he will also reap."[3] These are God's laws, and He will not lift those laws when we sin this way. In fact, He will discipline us all the more because He does not want us to ruin our physical, emotional, or spiritual health.

How, then, do we take care of ourselves? Let's look at the three key areas individually.

TAKING CARE OF YOUR BODY

Mark Twain's wife was always after the humorist to take better care of himself physically. Yet Twain remained a recalcitrant, unrepentant disciple of the principle, Do what you want and forget the rest. On one occasion he was supposedly relaxing on the porch when an elderly man passed briskly by on his daily walk around the neighborhood. Twain's wife remarked, "Look at him! Eighty years old and he's as spry as a boy. And do you know why? Because he takes long walks every day!"

Twain sat up and regarded the ancient man. He finally conceded, "He looks pretty fit at that. I must remember to do that myself when I am eighty."

Twain maintained, "The only way to keep your health is to eat what you don't want, drink what you don't like, and do what you'd druther not." Even in the early 1900s, people spoke of health in terms of food, drink, and activities that seemed unappealing.

In the 1980s and '90s, "taking care of myself" became a religious mantra. Americans concentrated on their health: jogging, running, and Nautilus routines rather than sitting on the porch watching life go by. Veggies and fruits rather than beef, pork, and eggs. In fact eggs became regarded as being almost as dangerous as live grenades! Many food labels claim, "low cholesterol" or "cholesterol free" or "low fat" because of our obsession with ridding our diet of fat and cholesterol. Yet heart disease is at an all-time high.

What would I recommend as a doctor and a psychiatrist? A simple diet and lifestyle. As a diabetic I have had to follow a rigorous, very limited diet all my life. And yet I often feel as if I'm living life abundantly. A healthy lifestyle doesn't have to be filled with dullness and deprivation. Much of physical fitness is simple common sense. Here are some guidelines to help you live this kind of simple but healthy life.

1. Eat right, eat a variety of foods, and above all, eat breakfast.

Strangely enough, one of the most often skipped meals among Americans is the one meal that will make us feel good all day, a decent breakfast. It only needs to be a bowl of cereal, but it can make or break a day.

Researchers have repeatedly proven that breakfast is the most important meal of the day. Why? Because at breakfast—literally "breaking the fast"— we get the nourishment that sustains us through most of the day. What we eat at lunch and dinner really doesn't benefit us until the day is almost over. But breakfast, being the first meal after eight or nine hours of "fasting," is absorbed rapidly and hits the bloodstream very quickly after consumption. It gives you strength from morning through the afternoon. And yet many people just skip it. They don't feel good in the morning, they say, claiming they're not "morning people." Or they offer some other excuse such as "food just doesn't taste good in the morning," and they knock down a couple cups of coffee, get a quick caffeine high and think that's sufficient. It isn't.

Simply start eating breakfast regularly—nothing too big that sits in your stomach, something simple and easily put together—and I guarantee you will feel better, perform better, and last longer each day. When some crisis strikes, you will be better prepared to deal with it effectively.

Beyond that, dietitians recommend a variety of foods: hamburger, pork, steak, fish, chicken, veggies, fruits, and everything else. Even snack foods now and then are not unhealthy. It's when one group is overemphasized that problems begin.

How does one lose weight and get into better shape? You don't need a special Hollywood, Scarsdale, or Liz Taylor diet. In fact, researchers have found that endless fad diets do more harm than good. No, getting into shape is not complicated: Eat in moderation, exercise in moderation, and keep your head clear!

It's that simple. The thing we most have to get over is our society's constant nagging through television commercials, billboards, magazines, and every other medium about how slim and trim and glamorous we should look. The funny thing is, the people in those ads don't even look like that in real life! Professionals spend hours making up every person who appears in an ad like that, and then the photo itself is "airbrushed" for its final look. Nothing is real!

Accepting our basic body shape and weight level—once we've made an honest effort to control our eating habits—is paramount. Some people are skinny; some are heavy. That's life. Where we fall on the chart was God's choice, not ours (unless we've fallen into the habit of overeating). Let's accept ourselves as we are and get off the diet merry-go-round!

If our minds are constantly on food, one of two things is wrong: We really aren't eating enough or, more likely, we don't have anything else that really interests us. Developing some real interests, especially in serving Christ, will go a long way to wrestle an eating problem into control.

Of course, this is not true across the board. Some people really are afflicted with a true disorder that will take more than willpower to break. (I recommend our books, *Love Hunger* and *The Love Hunger Weight-Loss Workbook* if you suspect you might be one of them.) But most of us—if we eat right, and that means three normal meals a day in descending volume (large breakfast, medium lunch, small dinner) with perhaps a small snack or two between lunch and dinner and after dinner—will feel far better.

If you feel a need to eat till you're full, try this:

- **Stock up on raw vegetables.** They're filling, nourishing, and they won't put on the fat.
- **Eat more slowly.** Psychologically if we'd just eat

more slowly and wait before taking that second helping, we'd feel better with less. Fast eaters actually consume more than they need because they don't give their bodies time to feel full.

- **Don't keep lots of junk food around.** If it's not there, you can't eat it!
- **Make a treat a treat.** Give yourself a bonus on occasion so that a special treat is really something special. That way it never loses its great taste.

God never intended food to become a compulsion for any of us. The cycle can be broken, but it must be approached the same way it began, step by step, little by little. Take it a day at a time and you will succeed.

2. Exercise and get the right amount of sleep.

Don't get into an exercise routine that you despise. The slogan, No pain, no gain, may be true, but by the same token, too much pain produces no gain because you'll give up.

The best exercise is simple. In the armed forces after basic training, short, maintenance exercises are performed in the morning and at night. It's nothing elaborate and many servicemen regard it as fun. I do my own version of these exercises, completing fifty push-ups and ten sit-ups every morning and then the same routine just before I go to bed.

Choose an exercise routine that fits you and can become a part of your schedule without constant sacrifice. (If you do an extensive program and your brain associates that routine with pain, you'll probably begin to dread it and finally give up.) If your exercise program takes more than a few minutes a day, it's probably not producing the benefits you want. Unless you're a bodybuilder, you don't need some daily regimen of an hour or two in the fitness center.

Beyond a few calisthenics each day, I'd recommend cultivating at least one or two year-round sports. Some people choose tennis, racquetball, swimming, and cycling because they can be done throughout the year in indoor facilities. Yet one of the very best forms of exercise is walking. It's easy, takes little effort, and is even highly pleasurable. You meet your neighbors, too, and you can do it virtually every day of the year. Some people even walk in malls to avoid the cold in winter and the heat in summer. Walking has tremendous cardiovascular benefits when done regularly, and it does not even need to be the "power-walking," which has become so popular. A brisk half-hour walk will raise your heart rate, get you breathing faster, and clear your mind. In fact, taking a walk during your lunch hour and then eating a light meal is a good alternative to eating a big lunch. Some companies have even opened indoor tracks for their employees because the benefits are so great.

Getting the right amount of sleep is also essential. The average person needs seven and a half to eight hours of sleep a night. Too little sleep can lead to hallucinations and a complete mental breakdown as has been discovered with soldiers who are pushed too hard in training and combat. Some people need more, some less; the key is consistency. And remember, one thing the Bible warns us against is carousing, staying up late, drinking, and the like. A party now and then is fine, but staying up late consistently will lead to a lack of discipline on many other fronts. When W. Somerset Maugham, the novelist, was asked the secret of his success, he said, "Every day I have done two distasteful things: In the morning I have gotten up, and at night I have gone to bed."

Not a bad plan for anyone.

3. Have a physical checkup.

Don't just see your doctor when you're sick. Get a physical at least once every two years. It's not failsafe, but it's often paid for by businesses or health benefits and is certainly worth the time and effort.

Eye exams are essential every few years, and dental checkups twice a year or so. The medical profession, contrary to popular belief, is not just out for the bucks; many doctors offer clinics during the year that are free or inexpensive.

It goes without saying that when something disturbs you—a nagging ache, a new pain in the back, blurry vision—you should see a doctor. Almost every known illness has a slow onset of symptoms and even the worst scourges known today are preceded by a lengthy series of indicators. If caught early enough, a multitude of common diseases and maladies are correctable. Avoid the belief that someone else should notice. You know more about yourself than anybody. If it's troubling, consult a doctor. Bite the bullet in terms of dollars. It's a small price to pay for genuine health. As some have said, good physical health not only adds years to your life, but life to your years.

4. Flee from sexual sin.

Our age is a maelstrom of sexually transmitted diseases. What is the cause? Not enough condoms? Not enough sex education? Not enough "safe sex"?

None of the above. It's sin. From fornication to adultery to all forms of perversity, there's no question that America's (and the world's) problem is sin. There are consequences of sin in the Bible from Adam and Eve to the Antichrist. Look at David's life: Everything was on the upswing until he sinned; then from the point of his adultery with Bathsheba and murder of her husband, it was all downhill. David was a "man after God's own heart," but even as much as God loved him, He did not mitigate the consequences of David's sin. God forgives. He forgets. He will never bring our sins up in eternity, and we cannot lose our salvation because of sin. But He warns us of the consequences again and again in Scripture. For example, "The wages of sin is death."[4]

Again, I cannot stress this enough. Sexual sin is a physical, mental, and spiritual killer. Disease, guilt, and the resulting separation from God put more people into doctors' offices than perhaps any other malady. Our world deceives itself with the belief that passing out condoms in schools, practicing so-called safe sex, and other remedies will help us. Satan is out there deceiving us all this minute, but those who rely upon the truth will break the odds. As Paul said, "Let no one deceive you by any means."[5]

Physical health is essential; so is mental health.

TAKING CARE OF YOURSELF EMOTIONALLY

A woman complained to a psychoanalyst, "My family thinks something is wrong with me simply because I like buckwheat cakes."

The analyst was puzzled. "But there's nothing wrong with liking buckwheat cakes. I like them myself."

"Oh, do you?" the woman answered, delighted. "You must come up someday. I have seven trunks full."

Most of us are not this unbalanced, but we do succumb to the three killer emotions. I deal with them every day in the clients I see in the counseling office: guilt, anger and its inevitable consequence, bitterness, and lust. Each one leads to whole panoplies of problems from depression to phobias, dysfunctions, and codependencies.

A hundred items could be tabulated as the essentials of mental health. But really only a few things are necessary. Solomon said, "As [a man] thinks in his heart, so is he,"[6] and he was right. How we think about ourselves, our lives, and others is the key. Let me give you a mental checklist designed specifically to help you beat the odds.

___ 1. Memorize Scripture.

You might think this would fall under spiritual health, but I put it here for a specific reason: Memorization and meditation on Scripture is largely a mental activity, and it contributes greatly to one's mental welfare. What does memorization do?

It sharpens your mind and your concentration. Learning God's Word and understanding it helps you become more direct in your approach to life. It helps you learn to think through activities and decisions as you face them. Memorization will train your mind.

It teaches you to think logically and directionally. The simple act of memorization puts thoughts in your mind and channels them. It helps you to see the world as God sees it. It focuses your spiritual and mental "eyes."

It raises your capacity for facts and truths. Strangely enough, the more you memorize, the more you can memorize. There is no saturation point. You find that your brain has a nearly limitless capacity for absorbing data. Studies have shown that memorization actually helps students get better grades and formulate better study habits.

It helps us combat the lies of the world, the flesh, and the devil. There are a multitude of falsehoods out there from "I'm worthless" to "God can't love me like He loves others" to "some sins just can't be overcome." As we memorize Scripture we are exposed to God's truth. Isaiah said God's Word [His truth] never returns void without accomplishing what it was sent out for.

___ 2. Be willing to love.

Real mental health is greatly strengthened by receiving and giving love in appropriate, honorable, and specific ways. "Love will cover a multitude of sins," Peter said.[7] Through love we reach out, give, share, open our hearts to others, become vulnerable, sacrifice—in fact love makes possible every positive trait of human character. Love like this was evident in the life of Peter Miller, a Baptist pastor who lived during the American Revolution.

Miller had a mortal enemy named Michael Wittman, an evil-spirited man disliked by nearly everyone. In a short time, Wittman was tried for treason, found guilty, and sentenced to die. Miller learned of the event and walked seventy miles on foot to Philadelphia to appeal to George Washington to spare the traitor. After making his case, Washington told Miller, "No, I cannot grant you the life of your friend."

Miller exclaimed, "My friend! He's the bitterest enemy I have!"

Washington was astonished. "You've walked seventy miles to save the life of an enemy?" There was a pause and then he said, "That puts the matter in a different light. I'll grant your pardon."

Miller took Wittman home as a friend.

Many people who live resentful, bitter lives because of what others have done to them find real transformation through love. The Scriptures say,

- "Love your enemies."
- "Pray for those who . . . persecute you."
- "Do not avenge yourselves."
- "Bless those who curse you."[8]

Why? Because it sets the mind and spirit free from the acids that bitterness and anger release in us. Love is the cornerstone of true mental health.

___ 3. Take time to laugh.

Take time to enjoy life. Dr. William Menninger, the founder of the famous Menninger Clinic in Minnesota, said, "Your mental health will be better if you have lots of fun outside of that office."

All the positive emotions—love, joy, peace, mirth—release into our bodies chemicals called endorphins and enkephalins that give us that tranquilizing, joyous effect.

Laughter heals where other emotions can cause harm. Norman Cousins, the well-known editor of *The Saturday Review of Literature* and author of *The Anatomy of an Illness*, believed he could wage war against his own struggle with illness by exposing himself to all forms of humor and laughter. He watched funny movies and TV shows, listened to humorous radio scripts, read humor and gathered around him people with a natural humorous bent. In the end, he won against the disease, and he believed laughter had healed him. Statistics have demonstrated that morose, high-strung, angry people live shorter lives than happy, joyous people.

Abraham Lincoln was renowned for his humor and storytelling. One of the jokes around Washington during his presidency told of a discussion between two Quaker women. One of them said that Jefferson Davis was sure to win the Civil War because he was a "praying man." The other Quaker replied, "But Mr. Lincoln is also a praying man."

"Yes," replied the first, "but God always thinks he's joking."

In the cabinet meeting that preceded the issuing of the Emancipation Proclamation, Lincoln read a droll chapter from a book by Artemus Ward, a famed humorist of the age. The cabinet members were all rather shocked that Lincoln would open such a proceeding with levity. No one laughed. Lincoln noted their response and said, "Gentlemen, why don't you laugh? With the fearful strain that is upon me night and day, if I did not laugh, I should die; and you need this medicine as much as I do."

Arnold H. Glasow said, "Laughter is a tranquilizer with no side effects."

Find reason to laugh. If you have none, look for something worth laughing at—a humorous movie, a theatrical performance, a recording, a sermon with plenty of humor in it. As Solomon said in Proverbs 17:22, "A merry heart does good."

___ 4. Face your fears.

Whatever you fear, face it. With time, fear only snowballs and grows larger. What looked small but scary at first can loom terrifying and awful in time if it is not faced and forced out.

There is a story of a man who kept a tiger. At first the tiger was young and playful, but as it grew it became fierce and confrontative. Soon it was uncontrollable. The man tried everything, but eventually he found only caging the tiger in a deep pit eliminated his fear of the animal. And then the tiger roared all night with anger and fury. The man was at his wit's end, but one day he had an idea. He went down into the pit as the tiger roared and stared the tiger in the eye. The tiger stopped roaring. He stared harder, more formidably. The tiger stopped pacing. It sat down. He walked over to it, looked it in the eye and said, "I will keep you with me now wherever I am. But now you know who is the master." The tiger put its tail between its legs and followed the man out of the pit, then lay down at the foot of his bed and slept.

This can be the story of any fear; as we face it, we find it is not as strong as it appeared. The fear may never go away, but we have mastered it.

John said, "There is no fear in love; but perfect love casts out fear."[9] How is that so? When we know we are loved by the omnipotent God, we realize there is nothing that can oppose us or fell us. We may even be killed in this world, but we know we have a permanent home in the next.

___ 5. Accept yourself as you are.

There is a saying in psychiatric circles: Change what can be changed and accept the rest. I see so many people whose lives would be improved dramatically by one basic ingredient: self-acceptance. Elements of your personality; handicaps; some illnesses; certain weaknesses and even strengths; your hair, nose, ears—everything about you that comes with the package from God must be accepted as His good gift.

How do you accept yourself that way? First, recognize God in His wisdom and love made you as you are. That cannot be changed. I have diabetes. I wish I didn't, but much good has come from it. Had I not gotten diabetes, I might never have left my father's farm in Arkansas. I'm sure I would have had an excellent life, but how many more people have been helped through the counseling ministry and work God has given me? Today, I can thank God for diabetes because I'm convinced without it I would not have become the person I am today.

The first step to acceptance is looking at yourself as God made you and giving thanks. The next is to do that every day, every hour, until it becomes a reality. If you do that, no other steps are necessary!

___ 6. Refuse to worry.

I was working on a book called *Worry-Free Living* and frankly I was worried—not about the book so much, but the weather. My friend and I were driving to the Dallas-Fort Worth Airport in a rainstorm so heavy we could hardly see the road in front of us.

My friend tried to encourage me. "Come on, Frank, the weather will be fine. We'll be able to take off okay, and we'll land in Atlanta in no time. You can finish writing the book during the plane ride."

I didn't feel like flying in this kind of weather. It was just the kind of weather I enjoy most when I'm in a warm bed, listening to the sound of the rain on the rooftop. "I don't know," I answered. "The weather sure looks bad to me—certainly not worry free." I have always hated to fly, especially in bad weather. After a long, treacherous ride over slick roads we arrived at the airport and boarded our plane.

The pilot came over the speaker, "Ladies and gentlemen, we have been detained. This is a terrible thunderstorm, but don't worry. We'll get you out of here before too long."

"Don't worry? Get me out of here?" I mumbled.

Finally he announced that our plane had been cleared for takeoff. We taxied down the runway and ascended into the black sky. The rain was heavy. Thunder seemed to burst all around us. I was "concerned" (an understatement, to say the least) so I decided to divert my attention and write the final chapter of the book, which now seemed to have a rather impractical title, considering our situation.

Worry-free living? How was that possible in storms like this one?

A sharp *craaaacck!* broke my thoughts. Then with a roar and a blinding flash, lightning hit the right wing of our plane. My stomach tightened, and I took in great gulps of air.

"Worry free? What am I doing on this crazy plane in a thunderstorm writing a book on being worry free?"

My friend just laughed. "Maybe so you can see if our theories really work!"

Okay, I thought. *I believe: You can—if you believe you can. So I'll believe that I can be worry free, even five miles above the ground in a violent thunderstorm. I will refuse to worry.*

In the next half hour I did manage to concentrate on reading the last draft of the book, every so often glancing out the window or grabbing the armrest to steady myself as the plane bumped and bounced through the choppy air. Most of all I frequently repeated Philippians 4:6: "Be anxious for nothing, but in everything by prayer and supplication, with thanksgiving, let your requests be made known to God"—one of the major verses we quote in *Worry-Free Living.*

And obviously we did land safely.

A certain amount of worry in life is normal. Stage fright is normal for those who must stand up in front of a crowd and speak. If you receive a menacing phone call at 1 A.M. you will naturally be worried. And yes, some apprehension when you are caught in a violent thunderstorm is natural. But the vast majority of worry that becomes neurotic is simple "dog-chasing-tail" mental activity.

What is the antidote to worry? Knowing God. Knowing who He is, what He is like, where He's taking you. If you know all that, how can you be worried?

___ 7. Give everyone, including yourself, a break.

Hey, we're all sinners. We make mistakes. If something is serious enough to require a confrontation or church discipline, then plow ahead. But most of the things we get angry about in life aren't worth the trouble. Learn to give people a break. Don't require perfection from your family, your spouse, your children, your parents. If real sins have been committed, talk them out and forgive. If you can change it, do so. Otherwise, just cut your friends and enemies some slack. Sinners sin. Don't expect anything less, and if you get more, then just thank God for His graciousness.

___ 8. Give problems time.

Many problems in life do not have quick, easy solutions. Some take years to solve. Some will never be solved. The Type A person may get things done, but he or she will also find a faster exit from life. Learn patience. In fact, how do we learn patience but by being patient in the face of insurmountable problems?

___ 9. Watch closely how you allow yourself to be entertained.

Television is the most powerful resource of the modern lifestyle. It's also a dangerous one. Regardless of what some researchers say, television and the media influence people—their values, their attitudes, their decisions. If this isn't so, why do so many corporations rush to use it to advertise their wares? What men see Tim Taylor doing on *Home Improvement*, they want to emulate. It's a normal response. What women and children see on *Roseanne* and *Murphy Brown*, they will imitate. It's a basic law of human nature: We learn to do by watching others.

I honestly recommend that every man and woman reading these pages assess his or her television-viewing habits. Are you throwing your life away day after day, night after night, watching sitcoms and soaps? Are you losing precious minutes of family life, sharing, giving, and serving in the hours you spend in front of the TV?

If the Music Man came around today he would not be talking about pool tables with a capital P that rhymes with T, and that spells "trouble!" No, he'd be saying, "A capital T followed up by a V, that spells "victim." Don't become a statistic in front of the boob tube. Ration those hours and use what you have left for family life, games, going out into the neighborhood, showing hospitality, and giving. You will never regret the loss.

Mental health is not an impossibility for the vast

majority of Christians. Some, yes, will require counseling and help to achieve real health. But God is gracious and good. He can do the impossible.

Dr. Willard S. Krabill, put it this way: "Someone has said that those who are mentally and emotionally healthy are those who have learned when to say Yes, when to say No, and when to say Whoopee!"[10]

God wants us to enjoy Him and the good life He has given us. He has given us the tools in the Spirit, the Word, prayer, and His people. Now we must employ them all in our lives to succeed.

TAKING CARE OF YOURSELF SPIRITUALLY

Several years ago a survey revealed that the average Christian prayed only three minutes a day and the average pastor only seven minutes. As a Christian, I say that is a travesty. As a psychiatrist, I say that is deeply troubling. The famous secular psychiatrist C. G. Jung once said there was nothing wrong with any of his patients that a religious worldview would not heal.

I see so many Christians talking about being Christians but doing little to live like Christians. As a doctor, I see this as being even more deleterious than atheism, agnosticism, or some other religion. Why? Because a non-Christian can at least have a semblance of health if he or she follows basic commonsense principles of life. But a Christian who does not practice his or her Christianity is making a double error, first by thinking that just "being" a Christian is enough and second by thinking that God is pleased. Chances are if a Christian does not practice his or her beliefs, God is seriously displeased!

What are the basic ingredients of a healthy spiritual life? Prayer, Bible study and meditation, fellowship. We looked at those in Chapter 3. Several other elements of the Christian life are also essential to keep our spiritual health: forgiveness, confession of sin, evangelism, and worship.

FORGIVENESS

Jesus spoke some formidable words about forgiveness in Matthew 6, right after introducing His disciples to the Lord's Prayer. He said, "For if you forgive men their trespasses, your heavenly Father will also forgive you. But if you do not forgive men their trespasses, neither will your Father forgive your trespasses."[11] There is more reason here for this command than just a divine law. When we fail or refuse to forgive we bottle up all kinds of potent negative emotions that will seep out of our lives in the form of irritability, nastiness, rejection, and resentment. Such emotions poison our relationships and destroy our ability to know and love God.

Charles Williams wrote in *The Forgiveness of Sins*, "Many reconciliations have broken down because both parties have come prepared to forgive and unprepared to be forgiven." Most relationships in life would be vastly improved by the simple act of forgiveness going both ways.

How do you forgive? Simply by making a choice. The expression, Forgive and forget, is a truism, but many wonder how it can be done. It's not that difficult. It doesn't mean you literally forget entirely an incident, but it means you choose not to dwell on a sin or wrong when it comes to mind.

Clara Barton, the founder of the Red Cross, was once asked if she remembered a particular incident in which someone severely wronged her. The friend exclaimed, "You mean you don't remember that time she . . . ?" Clara answered, "I distinctly remember forgetting that one."

Obviously, she hadn't entirely forgotten it as if it had never happened, but she refused to turn it over and over in her mind and let the resentment percolate. Forgiving is an act of will.

In *The Freedom of Forgiveness* David Augsburger wrote, "Forgive immediately, forgive continually, and then forgive—finally. Forgive once for all. End it with finality. Forgive forgetfully. It was said of Lincoln, 'His heart had no room for the memory of a wrong.' "[12]

CONFESSION OF SIN

The apostle James pointed out how important confession is when he said, "Confess your trespasses to one another, and pray for one another, that you may be healed."[13] Daily, even hourly, confessing of wrongs—as soon as you have committed them—is essential. William James, the eminent pragmatist and psychologist of the last century, said, "For him who confesses, shams are over and realities have begun."

Sir William Osler, Canadian physician and professor of medicine, said, "'Undress,' as George Herbert says, 'your soul at night,' not by self-examination, but by shedding, as you do your garments, the daily sins whether of omission or commission, and you will wake a free man, with a new life."

I often recommend my patients spend some time each night in review and confess anything the Holy Spirit brings to mind as sin. In some cases, going to the person you have sinned against and asking for forgiveness is also necessary. Obviously, this is required when you have really hurt someone with your words or actions.

But how do you determine whether to go when the other person may not know about your sin? Ask yourself, "Will there be more harm in his or her knowing my sin? Do I really need to tell him or her?" Some patients develop neuroses where they have to confess every evil thought or idea that pops into their heads. They become incessant "confession machines" who accomplish nothing except to make others feel sorry for them, or worse. Be careful in confessing sinful thoughts to others. Keep that between you and God.

EVANGELISM

Jesus told the disciples, "You shall be witnesses to Me."[14] His last command to all of us was to "go . . . and make disciples of all the nations."[15] While some Christians have a spiritual gift for evangelism, every Christian is called to be a witness. Statistics show that new Christians share their faith more in their first two years than they will the whole rest of their lives. There are many reasons for this from a psychological and spiritual point of view, ranging from the inevitable lack of contact with non-Christians as the new Christian builds new relationships to the waning of commitment as he or she slides into the routine of Christian faith.

But that doesn't excuse us. Dwight Moody, well-known evangelist and founder of Moody Bible Institute, had a policy of sharing his faith with at least one person every day. It's said that on some occasions when he reached the end of his day without having spoken to anyone about Christ he would rush out of his hotel room and find someone to speak to. When criticized about some of his unorthodox methods, he replied, "I like the way I do it better than the way most people don't do it."

Find a method that suits you and use it as the Lord gives you opportunity. Ask the Lord to open doors in your family, among your friends, and at work. Let the Spirit love others through you, and inevitably you will find a door opening here and there that you didn't expect.

WORSHIP

According to the Westminster Shorter Catechism, the whole reason we exist in this world is that we might "glorify God and enjoy Him forever." That is as fine a definition of what worship is all about as I've ever seen. Daniel Baumann said, "Worship is a stairway on which there is movement in two directions: God comes to man, and man comes to God." Worship is the meeting place of God and His people.

Brother Lawrence, the seventeenth-century monk who wrote the book *The Practice of the Presence of God*, said, "The end we ought to propose to ourselves is to become, in this life, the most perfect worshipers of God we can possibly be, as we hope to be, through all eternity."

We've heard those truths all our Christian lives. Many of them add up to less than minutes a day. And yet each is desperately important.

Dr. J. Wilbur Chapman, famed Christian author and evangelist, often spoke of his "rule for Christian living." He said, "The rule that governs my life is this: 'Anything that dims my vision of Christ, or takes away my taste for Bible study, or cramps my prayer life, or makes Christian work difficult, is wrong for me, and I must, as a Christian, turn away from it.'"

Not a bad thought at all.

That is the outlook that meets the odds with resourcefulness and valor. As we pray hourly and meditate on the Word, serving by giving a compliment here and an exhortation there, worshiping a moment as we watch a blue jay alight—however we do it—as we draw on that infinite ocean of grace that God promises us every moment of the day, we can beat the odds summarily. All of us will find our own way of conducting our lives. I've given you some suggestions gleaned from years of working in counseling, medicine, and in studying personal habit patterns. I know these ideas work. Take them as they're given: as heartfelt advice that can improve your life and help you overcome the difficulties you face. Taken this way, I am confident you and I will succeed for the Lord together.

CHAPTER 5

The Palm of His Hand

 Know That God Is with You

In 1989 the curtain between life and death seemed to raise all too often for my loved ones. It all began one day when Bonnie Tinker called and said, "Tink is dead. I hated to tell you, but I knew he would want you to know."

Erwin Tinker—his friends called him Tink—was the godliest man I had ever known. He had spent countless hours helping me to grow in Christ; he had been my leader and my mentor, and now he was gone. The grief was a deep inner pain I had never encountered before.

Not too long after that I was speaking at my publisher's sales conference when my secretary called with an urgent message: "Frank, call home immediately." I knew from the alarm in her voice something was wrong; my intuition told me I had lost my best friend. When I called home, my fears were confirmed: My mother had died that day in her sleep.

I felt totally crushed. My heart ached. I felt beaten, overwhelmed, and destroyed by the odds. She had been the one who had always told me I could overcome even the hardest opposition. She had first used the expression that came to mean so much in my life: "Frank, anyone who will try in Christ can beat the odds." She had been at my side through most of my troubles and had always believed in me. Now she was gone, and my heart hurt beyond anything I could put into words.

And then, as if the world were turning upside down, another call came. My father-in-law had died. "Mr. Holt went home to be with the Lord," Mary Alice's aunt told me. I had watched him fight a deadly lymphoma for twenty years, and he had won physically against tremendous odds with more courage and dedication than any man I had ever known. But it had finally beaten him.

When her dad died, Mary Alice was pregnant with our fourth child, and I feared for her health. She attended the funeral, but then developed symptoms that threatened a miscarriage. We both knew the baby could not survive if born that prematurely. The doctor put her to bed, and I encouraged her to hang in there. Drawing on the same resources we had learned and used as Christians for so many years, she fought back gallantly and carried the baby to term. Our daughter Alicia (we call her Allie) was healthy; her birth was like a breath of fresh air in the midst of all the death. Perhaps Alicia had been sent by God to fill the vacuum created by our losses.

But then another call came. "Frank, the Lord just made a house call," the voice said over the phone. This time it was my father. He was an old, tough, battle-hardened Christian, perhaps one of the last of his breed, a real country doctor.

We had done so much together. In many ways, we fought side by side in the battle of this life. Together, we had seen many victories and had truly beaten the odds. But there are no odds on death. Ultimately, it wins every time. And now, my truest and longest-running hero was gone.

I was in inner turmoil, suffering an anguish and agony I had never known. *Can I go on?* my heart cried out times without number. And inside, the same heart would respond, *Yes, I must go on for Christ.* Tink, Mother, my father-in-law, and Dad were all sent by God the Father to me, my family, our world. They had faithfully proclaimed His story. They would want me to do the same. I knew I had to go on—for Christ and in Christ.

To some that will sound trite, contrived. But I have known so many people for whom Christ is the answer, the only answer. Tink and my dad were my heroes in this life. Jesus gave them to me to provide hope, insight, and guidance, and to set a godly example. But Jesus is the Lord for all of us. Through Him I knew I would see Tink, my mom and dad, and Mr. Holt again, and we would be with Jesus forever.

That is a hope grounded in truth and fact. He's the key to everything, the key to overcoming all odds. With Him anything is possible. Without Him, this world is only a graveyard.

The real power and glory of Christianity can be summed up in the words of Colossians 1:27: "Christ in you, the hope of glory."

God, through Christ, dwells in us. Wherever we are, He is. We cannot flee into the pit to get away from Him or storm heaven to assault Him. He will never desert us. He is with us always, even to the end of the age.

We do not go up against any odds without His incredible support behind each of us. What is that support? Let me catalog some of the forces that stand behind us as we face trouble and distress in this world.

GOD HIMSELF IS WITH YOU

Of course, the first and most obvious truth is that God Himself is with us. Jesus said in Matthew 28:20, "I am with you always." The writer to the Hebrews assured us, speaking for God, "I will never leave you nor forsake you."[1] Study the Psalms and you find many of them opening with despair; but as the psalmist cries out in his fear he turns to God, and God's presence gives him assurance. When Moses had been in the wilderness for forty years and God appeared to him in the burning bush, God commissioned him to go back to Egypt and lead Israel to freedom. Moses balked, repeatedly throwing up reasons he himself was incapable.

- "Who am I?" he asked. "How can I complete such a monumental task?"
- "What if they do not believe me? Or believe that the Lord appeared to me?"
- "But I am not eloquent. I am slow of speech."

Each time God assured him that it was not he who would be doing it; no, God Himself would be there. He even gave Moses two signs that would prove His power and presence: Moses' staff turned into a snake when thrown to the ground, and Moses' hand was smitten with leprosy when he placed it in his cloak.

The Old Testament, however, does not tell us that God's Spirit was a permanent presence in the lives of the saints. In the New Testament, though, we do have that great assurance. God is inside us and remains with us. He has in fact, sealed us with His blood, as Ephesians 1:13 says. The apostle Paul reminded the Corinthians of this when they were tempted by sexual immorality. "Do you not know that your body is the temple of the Holy Spirit who is in you, whom you have from God?"[2]

Paul told the Romans, "the Spirit Himself bears witness with our spirit that we are children of God."[3] This is a special reality that only the Christian can claim. God dwells in us and speaks to us daily, assuring us we are His and that He is with us. When Jesus was in the Garden of Gethsemane the night before the Cross, he addressed His Father as *Abba,* the Aramaic term for "Daddy," the familiar, childlike name for "father."

But that's not the only time *Abba* is used in the Bible. The apostle Paul used the term in two different letters to early churches. He told the Roman Christians, "For as many as are led by the Spirit of God, these are sons of God." Then he encouraged them to cry out to God, using "Abba, Father."[4] *Daddy.* Again in Galatians 4:6, he told Christians they were sons of God. "And because you are sons," he said, "God has sent forth the Spirit of His Son into your hearts, crying out, 'Abba, Father!' " *Daddy.* God is personal, very near, very real, like a father, says Paul. Our Daddy.

There is a story of an orphan boy who had a terrible stutter, and all the doctors saw no way to cure him. Then one evening when he was asked to say grace at dinner, the boy prayed. He didn't stutter once, giving a short but sincere prayer of thanks. Everyone was astonished, and one of the headmasters went to the boy and asked him why he didn't stutter. "Because I was speaking to G-God," he said with the familiar stutter starting up.

"But why does that make a difference?" he was asked.

"Because God loves me," the boy answered.

The fact that God not only loves us but is in us, with us, and around us, going ahead and behind us in life, is tremendous assurance. Even when times come that we can't "feel" Him, as in those times of depression or anxiety, God is there. He never leaves us. This presence means we never face the odds alone.

The inventor of the telegraph, Samuel B. Morse, was once interviewed by pastor George Hervey. Hervey inquired, "Professor Morse, when you were making your experiments at the university, did you ever come to a standstill, not knowing what to do next?"

"Oh, yes, more than once," Morse replied.

"Then what did you do?"

"I've never discussed this with anyone, so the public knows nothing about it. But now that you ask me, I'll tell you frankly—I prayed for more light."

"And did God give you the wisdom and know-how you needed?" Hervey continued.

"Yes, He did. That's why I never felt I deserved the honors that came to me from America and Europe because of the invention associated with my name. I had made a valuable application of the use of electrical power, but it was all through God's help. It wasn't because I was superior to other scientists. When the Lord wanted to bestow this gift upon mankind, He had to use someone. I'm just grateful He chose to reveal it to me."

What was the first message that Morse sent over that telegraph? Undoubtedly, you've heard of it: "What hath God wrought?"[5]

God's presence is real. Millions can attest to it. Through that presence, Morse overcame the odds and invented the telegraph. I believe it can be the same for us.

GOD'S SUPERNATURAL PEACE IS WITH YOU

A second source of power and confidence for beating the odds is God's supernatural peace. Paul wrote in Philippians, "Be anxious for nothing, but in everything by prayer and supplication, with thanksgiving, let your requests be made known to God; and the peace of God, which surpasses all understanding, will guard your hearts and minds through Christ Jesus."[6] The antidote for anxiety is God's peace. But the first step is "prayer and supplication, with thanksgiving." Spend time in prayer about a problem and God's promise is that He will give you His peace.

I have seen this work in many miraculous ways in

people who were deeply afraid and depressed. But I have also counseled people who seem to find God's peace elusive. They can't seem to "get it," and this troubles them.

I think part of the answer is that God's peace is not always His answer for us at that time. Sometimes He allows us to go through troubles to force to the surface doubts and anxieties He wants us to deal with before we can feel His peace again. That may mean some real work on the counselee's part. It may mean days and weeks of prayer and seeking God, applying principles, and working through a serious problem.

On occasion a darkness seems to envelop some people and no matter how hard they try and labor, there is no peace. Again, God may be training and testing us through mortal trials that draw us out to the limit. Giving us that peace in the midst of it is not His purpose.

Paul spoke of how he was stretched to the maximum: "We were burdened beyond measure, above strength, so that we despaired even of life."[7] Then he told how God's comfort came to him so he could comfort others. Sometimes God allows us to go through severe emotional, spiritual, and physical trials simply so we can help others in similar situations. Any psychiatrist knows the power of a kindred spirit, one who has gone through what the counselee has gone through. Often in group therapy I am unable to help someone, but a fellow patient who has experienced (or is experiencing) what the patient is going through can say just the right thing.

God's peace is not a magic elixir or an amulet you rub through prayer and supplication. It is a reality that we can count on when God sees its necessity. The ultimate source of peace, though, is His Word. In it He lets us know His plans for us, for the world, and for all His people. Jesus told His disciples the night before He was crucified, "These things I have spoken to you, that in Me you may have peace. In the world you will have tribulation; but be of good cheer, I have overcome the world."[8] God's peace is bound up in faith in Christ and what He has said. As we learn to lean and depend and trust in Him, no matter what the world is doing outside, we learn true peace.

Philip Yancey, author of *Where Is God When It Hurts?*, has written, "When we have nothing else to lean on, not even ourselves, He is still there."[9]

Thornton Wilder's play *Our Town* has a scene in which Rebecca Gibbs talks to her brother George. Rebecca says, "George, do you know what Jane Crowfoot's minister wrote to her when she was sick, the minister in the town church back in the town from which she came? He wrote a letter to her and addressed the envelope in a strange way."

"What did he write?" George asks.

"He wrote, 'Jane Crowfoot, Crowfoot Farms,

Grover's Corners, Sussex County, New Hampshire, United States of America.'"

"Well, what's so funny about that?"

"Well, that's not all," Jane answers. "United States of America, Western Hemisphere, Planet Earth, Solar System, the Universe, the mind of God."

The mind of God! Do you know that you and I are always in God's mind, and not just thought about, but loved, nurtured, cared for, spoken of with reverence and concern? For every Christian, God is near, a ready presence in time of need!

GOD'S ANGELS ARE WITH YOU

God's angels are a third part of His special presence, one we often overlook because they seem so mystical, although authors like Billy Graham and Frank Peretti have popularized their existence in recent years. And a new book, *Celebration of Angels,* by Timothy Jones, associate editor of *Christianity Today,* gives a very complete picture of how God ministers to us through His angels.

One of the great examples of an angel's presence in the Bible is found in 2 Kings 6. In that passage, the king of Aram pursues Elisha because the king realizes Elisha is able to predict every move the king is making to overcome Israel. So the king goes after the prophet. Eliminate him, the king thinks, and he can control the Israelites.

As Elisha and his servant Gehazi stop overnight to sleep in Dothan, the king comes up with his army and surrounds the city. Gehazi awakens first. He goes out and sees the king's tremendous forces and knows all is lost, so he runs to Elisha and tells him. Elisha answers, "Do not fear, for those who are with us are more than those who are with them."

Gehazi doesn't understand, so Elisha prays that God will open Gehazi's eyes. What does Gehazi see once his eyes are opened? The text says, "The mountain was full of horses and chariots of fire all around Elisha." An army of angels! Then Elisha prays that God will strike the king's army with blindness, and God does so. Elisha leads these blinded soldiers to Samaria into the hands of the king of Israel!

The Bible is actually full of angels, which is one reason some modern thinkers scorn it as a "fanciful" book. Second Kings 19 describes how one angel killed 185,000 warriors of Assyria. Several times angels appeared to Daniel to deliver messages, and, of course, it was Gabriel who spoke with Mary and informed her she would be the mother of Jesus Christ. I wonder how often we do not see God's angels among us.

In his book *Angels: God's Secret Agents,* Billy Graham tells of the story of John G. Paton, missionary to the New Hebrides Islands. One night John's mission headquarters were surrounded by natives, determined to burn the missionaries out and kill them. Paton and his wife prayed in terror the whole night. In the morning, they were astonished to see their enemies depart. They thanked God for His deliverance, sure His providence had interceded.

A year later, after many in the tribe had converted to faith in Christ, Paton remembered the incident and asked the chief about it. "What made you leave in the morning without burning the mission station down or harming me or my wife?" he asked.

The chief was surprised. "Who were all those men you had with you there?"

Now it was Paton's turn to show surprise. "There were no men there," he said, "just my wife and I."

The chief told him they had seen hundreds of tall, gallant warriors encircling the refuge; the night shone with the light from their garments and the flaming swords in their hands. As the chief described the scene, Paton realized an angelic army had surrounded them. The chief agreed that was the only explanation.[10]

Graham tells other similar stories of remarkable visitations. A little girl came to a Dr. S. W. Mitchell of Philadelphia, reporting that her mother was ill and asking if he would come to help her. When Mitchell went to the woman, he found her terribly ill with pneumonia, but when he mentioned the little girl, he learned the girl had been dead nearly a month.

Norman Vincent Peale also told stories of angelic visitations. After months of work, a missionary who worked among a cannibalistic tribe in the South Sea Islands succeeded in converting the chief. One day in a time of fellowship, the chief said, "Remember the time you first came among us?"

"Indeed I do," replied the missionary. "As I went through the forest I became aware of hostile forces all around me."

"They did indeed surround you," said the chief, "for we were following you to kill you, but something prevented us from doing it."

"And what was that?"

"Now that we are friends, tell me. Who were those two shining ones walking on either side of you?"[11]

The Christian Reader carried this story from Rudy Friesen. Maria Pankratz and her daughter fled with a sister and other refugees from the Soviet Union into East Germany ahead of the retreating German army during World War II. They hid in a small apartment in Neustadt. One night a Russian soldier who had supplied them with food entered their apartment. Everyone was silent. Even the children hushed as the soldier looked around and sat down.

Later, there was a commotion outside and cursing. The apartment door was thrust open. Another soldier staggered into the room in a drunken rage.

The five women in the back pled with God for deliverance.

The soldier staggered forward, then abruptly stopped. He appeared to be trying to speak, but didn't. His whole body stiffened. Then as he gaped, the first soldier stood and led him away. The women heard them speak on the stairs. The second soldier said to the first, "What did those people do to me that I couldn't enter the room and I couldn't speak?"

"I don't know," the first said.

Today Mary Pankratz believes she and her friends were protected by an angel.[12]

A friend of mine tells me yet another story of a woman in his church who was at a prayer meeting and told the crowd that while she was driving that night, she came to a green light. Normally, she would just go through. But she said she had a "strange impulse" to stop and look both ways. As she put her foot on the brake, another van sped through the intersection, going through the red light and narrowly missing her car. She wondered if that was God's providence or if an angel had stopped her.

What can we make of these supernatural occurrences except that God does protect us and act in our world through His ministering spirits, angels? How often have we been protected from an accident or an attack or a difficult situation through the intervention of an angel? We may never know. Yet if one angel could kill off 185,000 Assyrians, what power they must possess!

GOD'S HEDGE SURROUNDS YOU

The last thing I want to mention is the hedge, a very personal spiritual wall that God puts up around us so we cannot be touched at certain times. It's only mentioned in Scripture in the book of Job, where Satan complains about God's placing a hedge about Job that kept anything from harming or molesting him in his business, family, or personal life.

Satan challenged God, saying, in effect, "If you remove the hedge from around Job, he will surely curse You to Your face." And God agreed to remove the hedge just as He may also allow the hedge around us to be lowered or even removed so that Satan is given some freedom to test us.

Several situations revealed in other Scripture references indicate this is true. First, there's the passage in Luke 22:31–34 where Jesus tells Peter he's going to deny Him three times. Peter protests, but then Jesus tells him that Satan has "asked for you, that he may sift you as wheat." The interesting thing about the passage is not just that God obviously gave Satan what he requested (the denial was the test, and Peter failed the test), but that Satan had to ask for it. Obviously, Satan couldn't touch Peter unless God granted him a special dispensation. Finally, Jesus told Peter, "when you have returned to Me, strengthen your brethren." Jesus was telling Peter first that Satan had asked for Peter and would get what he requested, but second, that Peter would fail the test. In other words, God let Satan do something to Peter even though God knew Peter would fail. The passage ends, however, with Jesus' telling Peter he would return to Him. It's a tough passage to understand, but the fact remains that God protected Peter in a special way under normal conditions.

Then there's the situation of King Saul in 1 Samuel 16:14 where "the Spirit of the LORD departed from Saul, and a distressing spirit from the LORD troubled him." Again, we see the transition from protection to nonprotection.

Finally, there's the story in 2 Corinthians 12:7–10 of God sending Paul a "thorn in the flesh" to keep him from exalting himself about the greatness of certain revelations he'd received earlier. Paul entreated the Lord three times to remove this influence, and God refused, telling Paul that "My strength is made perfect in weakness."

I suppose we cannot make too much of something that is not revealed in too great a depth in Scripture, but I'm convinced that there is a hedge for each of us that God uses to limit Satan's influence on us. I believe God has protected me spiritually from immoral conduct by surrounding me with His hedge.

In *The Screwtape Letters,* C. S. Lewis wrote that often when a person first converts to Christianity he is set free from certain long-term vices and habits that he could not extricate himself from on his own. There is this period, Lewis says, when we have a "honeymoon" with the Lord, a hedge, a special protection from God during our early nurturing period. God uses this to give us a good send-off, so to speak, and help us learn to walk with Him.

But inevitably, God has other things in mind, said Lewis, and He thrusts that Christian into steeper, harder elements of Christian living. That leads to the idea of the troughs, those harrowing periods in which one's faith and even one's life are sorely tested.

What then do all these elements of God's presence tell us? Several things . . .

GOD IS WITH YOU, SO YOU CAN . . .

God's presence, God's peace, and God's angels are with us, therefore we can . . .

1. Trust Him.

We Christians speak glibly of "trusting the Lord"

and "having faith" and "depending on Him," but this is the very bedrock of the Christian walk. It means we continue to believe God and His Word, regardless of how things look in the world around us. Trusting Him means continuing to go to Him in prayer, continuing to love and believe in and hope in Him even when everything in the world seems to be saying it's all an incredible hoax. How do you trust God? I believe it's an act of our will in which we expect Him to release His presence, His peace, and His angels.

For instance, if we're out of work, we choose to take action on the basis of His promise that He will meet our needs, that He will open a door somewhere. Trusting Him does not mean putting Him on a schedule, but at the same time it involves praying through realistic goals. It could involve such prayer as, "Lord, I'm going to give it my best shot to get a job within six months. If I can't find anything in that period, I'll believe You're leading me into another [career, city, plan of action]."

Or, if you and your spouse would like to have a baby but you've been unable to conceive, trusting Him might mean spending time in prayer, exploring the options, and seeking direction about what way to go.

Mary Alice and I had just such an experience during the third year of our marriage. Mary Alice experienced six weeks of severe menstrual pain so she went to the doctor and was amazed when he told her she was suffering a miscarriage (even though she hadn't realized she was pregnant). Within the next two years she had two more miscarriages.

Every medical book we read said that her chances of carrying a child to term became less likely with each miscarriage. One day we sat down together and decided, "With God's help, we can have a child." We would do everything we could, and then leave the rest to God.

After a few months Mary Alice became pregnant again. We decided she would spend the first three months resting—and maybe the entire nine months. The odds were against us, we knew. Yet at three months we were able to hear the baby's heartbeat.

At four months—the period when Mary Alice had previously lost two of the babies—she was still all right. At five months, she began wearing maternity clothes!

In the thirty-second week of her pregnancy, however, the doctor said Mary Alice was showing signs of premature labor, and he put her in the hospital. Every little pain frightened her because she was afraid it might lead to labor pains and the baby's premature birth. Still we trusted God.

Six weeks later the pains seemed to stop. The doctor sent Mary Alice home since the baby was now developed enough to survive. Two weeks later, on December 13, 1974, Rachel Marie Minirth was born, a healthy, bright-eyed, seven-pound, eleven-ounce girl! We had trusted God and He walked with us through every day of those long, trying eight months.

Trusting Him does not mean you never have doubts, worries, setbacks, or even moments when you must "retrust" God and reassert your faith after some kind of spiritual blowout. It does not mean you're so intrepid that not the smallest, faintest vestige of skepticism or uncertainty slips into your mind. Trust is a dynamic reality that is always in a state of flux, but at its foundation, when we really trust the Lord, it's the rock that we stand on whenever all else fails. Trust is the thing that is as embedded in us as we are in Him. We cannot escape it, and in the end true Christians will trust, even if they're not sure why they are doing it.

2. Feel His love.

If there is a single truth in the Bible meant to help us believe we have value as people, it's this: God's love is so great that He deigns to come dwell inside of us. He watches over us like the mother of a toddler moment by moment every day of our lives. He prepares the way ahead of us. He goes before us and makes sure no enemies are there to attack us. He puts up that hedge and fends off attacks we don't even know about.

But above all, He simply wants to be with us, to

be friends, to be part of our lives, to share everything. My wife and I have the closest relationship I
could ever imagine having with another human
being. And yet I know that in many ways a relationship between two human beings can never come
close to our relationship with the Divine. God
knows my thoughts before I even think them, as
Psalm 139 says. He knows my heart when I don't
know my heart. He has planned out my days so that
I might "walk" in all the "good works" He prepared
for us beforehand."[13] "I am fearfully and wonderfully
made."[14] God personally shaped every element of
my being while I was yet in the womb.

What can we say of all this personal attention? We
don't even give ourselves that kind of attention, and
yet God does it with all of us all our lives. He wants
to be with me, with you, with each of us.

Remember the division between kids who were
cool and "with it" in school and those who were
uncool, nerdy, twerpy, and so on. I remember being
on the latter side of that division for many years.
Because of my medical condition, I was never one
of the stars, as I mentioned in Chapter 1. And when
I found the almighty God, Creator of the universe,
not only wanted to save me but to be my best
friend, I was astonished. Then when it happened
and I found out it really was true, I was so overjoyed
and grateful I think in some ways I've never completely gotten over it. It's something none of us

should ever recover from. God loves us as if we were the only ones He had to love. And He regards us as friends whom He will introduce to the rest of the world with genuine joy and pride. There's no sense with Him that we might be uncool, or "not with it," or poor, or stupid, or anything like that. With Him, we're number one. Important enough to be with, and to protect, and to nurture, and to care for every day.

3. Know that nothing can touch you.

No one can touch you. No angel, demon, or human can attack, hurt, malign, or even cross paths with you unless God Himself has allowed it. And since God is wise, loving, holy, just, righteous, and perfect, you have every reason to trust that whatever does get through only got through because God allowed it for your ultimate good.

I don't know how that works out in every detail. I only know that as Romans 8:28 says, He causes "all things [to] work together for good," and as Ephesians 1:11 says, He "works all things according to the counsel of His will." The problem with this doctrine is that people try to apply it specifically to a situation and try to understand God's "purpose" or "plan" or "what He's doing" or "why He did this or that," and they get all mixed up. They can't see any good from a child who dies at an early age, or a friend smitten with AIDS from a blood transfusion (as the tennis pro Arthur Ashe was), and they conceive of any number of "unjust" situations that fly in the face of a good, loving God who is all-powerful.

The truth is that God does not offer explanations for each individual incident. He simply says, "Trust Me. I know what I'm doing. Nothing can touch you but what I allow, and I only allow those things I intend to work for good." People who want an explanation ask for something God can't give. Why? Because if we ask for an explanation of a God-sized problem, we're going to get a God-sized explanation. And we just aren't big enough for that.

Again, it comes down to trust. God really is working in our lives for good. No one can derail that process.

4. Take action.

The principle of God's sovereign care is not just meant to reassure us; it's meant to move us to action. Because we know He is with us and that He loves us and protects us, there are no real risks except when we act in clear disobedience to His revealed will. Ultimately, nothing can be stopped, just as John wrote in Revelation 3:7: God "opens and no one shuts," and "shuts and no one opens."

What happens when kings and commanders and the powerful make plans to overthrow God? Psalm

2:4 says God laughs at them. "The LORD shall hold them in derision."

Is there anyone who can subvert the plans and directives of God? Psalm 33:10-11 says, "The LORD brings the counsel of the nations to nothing; / He makes the plans of the peoples of no effect. / The counsel of the LORD stands forever, / The plans of His heart to all generations."

Because we have this powerful Person standing behind us, going before us, and ever planning the way, we have nothing to fear. There are no odds that can ultimately stop us.

Remember David and Goliath? What was it that impelled David? Faith? Yes, but faith in what, in whom? David had faith in a powerful God whom the "uncircumcised Philistine" had no right to taunt. He acted because he knew who God was and what He could do.

What about Moses? God asked—no, *commanded*—Moses five times to go to Egypt and speak with Pharaoh, and five times Moses refused. In the end, though, he finally went because he had no other choice. Moses was a weak, embittered, wimp of a human being. He didn't believe in himself, let alone God, even after God gave him powerful miracles to use to convince the people he was sent by an almighty Divinity. So what did God do? He entered Moses into His personalized program of confidence building and discipleship. He began performing miracle after miracle, showing Moses what awesome power He had wielded. He let Moses complain and ask to die, and then He sent Moses back to Pharaoh to perform another set of incredible miraculous feats. In time, Moses witnessed spectacle after spectacle; rivers that turned red with blood. Thousands of frogs. Lice. Livestock diseases. Boils. Locusts. Three days of darkness. And finally death to firstborn children. And every step of the way Moses found God standing by his side.

Thus it was that Moses stood on the edge of the Red Sea in Exodus 14, the chariots of Pharaoh whirring toward him. The Egyptians wanted Moses' head! Everyone was frightened, terrified. Everyone, that is, except one person. Moses. He cried, "Stand still, and see the salvation of the LORD."[15] Moses didn't even know what God was going to do, but finally he had faith. He knew God was not planning to let them die! He acted because He had seen the power, love, and goodness of God in action.

It was the same for the disciples. Before the Cross, they were brave at times. But when Jesus faced death, they scattered, terrified. Peter even denied knowing Jesus three times to slave girls and servants. Then Jesus arose; He appeared to them. They saw His power again exemplified in the most remarkable miracle of all, one they didn't understand or expect even though Jesus had told them about it numerous times. Jesus appeared at the most unanticipated moments over a period of forty days. They undoubtedly began to expect that He was around every corner, about to appear at every campfire or meeting. And thus, Jesus prepared them for the coming of the Spirit, the means by which He would actually indwell them.

When the Spirit came, what happened? Those disciples were galvanized. They spoke in languages they'd never learned. When the populace accused them of being drunk, Peter—who had only weeks before denied he even knew Jesus—stood and preached the greatest sermon perhaps of all time. Three thousand people were converted. Those disciples went on to turn the world upside down. Why? Because they knew God was inside them, this God who had done miracle after miracle. They went on to do the same deeds.

What was it that God's presence and power did to them? It made them bold, unafraid to take responsible risks. And that is what God's presence and power should do for us!

So as you face the dark, the pain, and the odds, remember this: You are not alone. God is with you. His peace is available, and His people can help you. Even now, spiritual forces surround us that are fighting on our behalf.

That casts the odds a little more in our favor, doesn't it?

Chapter 6

The Turning Tide

 *Never Give Up*

One day a few years ago I sat in a local bank, reaping the results of that poor financial decision I mentioned in Chapter 3. Paul Meier and I had cosigned a note for some buildings in Texas.

"Did you guarantee the bank notes on those buildings?" the banker asked me that day.

At first I tried to joke with the banker, which I learned is not a good idea when you owe a banker money. "No, it was actually my alter ego! He tries to pass himself off as me at times. But I didn't really . . ."

I finally murmured, "Of course I signed those notes. You know that."

"Your cosigner is going bankrupt, and you will be responsible for the buildings," the banker answered flatly.

My heart almost stopped beating. Real estate in

Texas had bottomed out. One of the buildings was in Austin; another was right down the street from our central offices in Richardson. Neither was fully occupied, and both were worth less on the current real estate market than had been paid for them.

One answer was to declare bankruptcy. Yet this was not really an option, I felt.

My dad had always told me that a good name was to be chosen over great riches, and that one way to keep a good name was to "always, always" act with integrity in regard to money issues.

I looked to the Bible to see what the Lord would have me do, and the Scriptures all seemed to increase my determination to stand firm despite the pressure:

- "I will not be afraid of ten thousands of people / Who have set themselves against me all around."
- "Be steadfast, immovable, always abounding in the work of the Lord."
- "Be strong in the Lord and in the power of His might."
- "Having done all, . . . stand."[1]

The same message is repeated all through the Scriptures: Endure. Persevere. Hang in there.

If a single principle is necessary in the battle to beat the odds, I would say it is this one: If you persevere, stick with your plan, and work hard, no matter what opposition or defeat assails you, sooner or later you will beat the odds. The odds are in favor of the persevering person because with every attempt at success, he or she lowers the odds one notch. Eventually, perseverance is going to lower those odds down to even!

How do you beat the odds? By persevering. When you suffer a financial setback, you come back. When you have the carpet pulled out from under you, you get up again. When the bottom caves in, you come out on the other side and then wriggle back up to the top. You beat the odds by coming back and coming back and coming back.

Over a hundred years ago, when the inventor Gail Borden crossed the Atlantic from England, the milk onboard ship happened to be contaminated, and two children died. Borden resolved to come up with a means of preserving milk for sea passage so it could be stored without becoming toxic. His solution was something he later called "condensed milk." You can still buy Borden's condensed milk in supermarkets today. His success, though, did not come easy. It took him many experiments and many attempts to find his solution. Today, his gravestone reads, "I tried and failed. I tried again and again and succeeded."

That's a simple picture of perseverance. Every invention that ever saw daylight, every artistic composition that now is framed and revered in museums throughout the world, every sermon that had an impact—all came to be for one reason: Someone persevered. Mrs. Leon R. Walters put it this way: "Lord, give me the determination and tenacity of a weed."[2]

James J. Corbett of boxing fame said, "Fight one more round. When your feet are so tired that you have to shuffle back to the center of the ring, fight one more round. When your arms are so tired that you can hardly lift your hands to come on guard, fight one more round. When your nose is bleeding and your eyes are black and you are so tired you wish your opponent would crack you on the jaw and put you to sleep, fight one more round—remembering that the man who fights one more round is never whipped."

That's success in a nutshell, both in history books and in the Bible.

Jesus sweat drops of blood in the Garden of Gethsemane. He pled to be released from His mission. But in the end He said, "Thy will be done." And He persevered to the moment when He cried, "It is finished."

Samson labored at the wheel, blind, forgotten, and overwhelmed by his own guilt and failure. But his chance came and as he stood before the Philistines who laughed at the "strong man of Israel" as they dined, he planted his hands on two pillars and brought down the house, killing more with his death than in his life.

Paul was beaten and jailed in Philippi. He went on to Athens, where he was scorned and laughed at. He continued on to Corinth, where he planted a church that became his greatest discipling problem and worry. But he kept on. Through one more missionary journey (there were three in all), he planted churches that would transform the Roman world.

What made these people who they were? One quality: perseverance.

How do you become a person who perseveres and overcomes the odds? Let me offer some thoughts that helped me as I faced that financial crisis.

A PLAN FOR PERSEVERANCE

I have always developed a written plan for any crisis in our family, and this time was no different. In the weeks after my meeting with the banker I worked through the same nine-step process I'd used so many times before. It's a process that's as valid today for your problem situation as it was back then for mine.

1. Decide what you're committed to.

The first step in achieving any goal in life is to decide what's worth pursuing. Only you can decide this. What is important to me probably won't be important to you, and vice versa. As I mentioned, integrity was more important to me than wealth. What is important to you? Weigh your priorities before you decide if you want to persevere.

I have a friend who was a pastor for a number of years and then left the pastorate in some pain and grief because he could not deal with his own lack of success and disappointment in his church's lack of growth. At the same time, he began pursuing another direction in life, writing articles, newsletters, and poetry for the Lord. He soon found that no amount of rejection from editors derailed him. In fact, such rejections were only spurs to get him to work harder. Today he is a successful author who knows his ministry for the Lord was always in writing, not pastoring.

You have to look at your life and figure out what you are unwilling to sacrifice. It might be a sport. It could be a business, a ministry, or a profession. Maybe it's an invention you've come up with or a process of discipleship you want to share with the world. Whatever it is, only you can determine if you're willing to pay the price to bring your dream to life.

Martin Luther made such a decision early in his life. He was infuriated by the Catholic church's practice of indulgences, which encouraged people to use their money to secure fewer years in purgatory for their dead relatives. This practice was epitomized by the statement, "The moment the coin into the chest doest clink the soul into purgatory doest cease to sink."

Why, he asked, do we have to pay this money if God could just free these souls anyway?

Eventually he posed these thoughts and others in an essay he called "Ninety-five Theses." Then he nailed the document to the door of Wittenberg Church, where people who wanted to debate an issue posted such invitations. On that day, Luther started a process that led to the Protestant Reformation.

At one point, the Diet of Worms (a group of men at the city of Worms who gathered to judge whether Luther's writings were heretical) determined that Luther's writings did not conform to the tradition of the church. He was warned to recant.

Luther made one response. As he stood before that august gathering of revered men of the church he said, "Unless I am convinced by Sacred Scripture or by evident reason, I cannot recant. For my conscience is held capture by the Word of God, and to act against conscience is neither right nor safe. Here I stand, I can do no other, God help me."

Those are the words of a man committed to a belief, a goal, a dream. He could not escape it. He could not run from it or forget it or give up on it.

During Martin Luther's lifetime he restored three great truths:

- The validity of "Scripture alone" (and not the words of men).
- The validity of "faith alone" (and not the works of men).
- The validity of "every man as a priest of God" (rather than the need for each of us to have the intercession of a special priest to know God).

He gave his life in defense of those beliefs.

To persevere against the odds is sometimes a matter of life and death!

2. Outline your goals.

Once you're sure you want to accomplish something in the face of towering odds, you need to set down some goals on paper. Dr. Howard Hendricks, a colleague of mine at Dallas Theological Seminary, often tells his students that the most important thing they can do during their time in seminary is to sit down and write out their goals. "If you don't know what you're aiming for, you'll hit it every time—and fail!"

In making our goals and plans, we must all look at the big picture.

I might want to build a hundred Minirth Meier New Life Clinics the world over, but if I don't take care of my health I'll never realize my dream. So when we consider goals, we have to get the big picture. If I want to give a million dollars to missions during my lifetime, I must go about making smaller and lesser goals within a large framework that will lead to that end.

How do you make goals? It's very simple. Make them specific, measurable, and reachable. "I want to give five thousand dollars to missions this year." That's specific. "I want to give to missions" is not.

Second, make them measurable. If my goal is to lose weight, then I should set a goal that I can literally measure. "I want to lose ten pounds this year." Then weigh yourself at the start and at the finish, and you know whether you reached it!

Third, make them reachable. I recommend a "faith-sized" goal, a goal that's small enough that you believe it can be done but also big enough that you know if God isn't involved, it won't happen. That's the faith part. You have to rely on God to get there. It's not just something you could do in your own strength.

In 1971, Willis Reed was the captain of the world champion New York Knicks basketball team. But in November of that year he had to quit because of tendinitis in his knee. Reed began a make-it-or-break-it struggle to remain in basketball. He began with one goal: to get back on the team and into the game. Then he broke it down into the exercises he'd have to do day by day to reach that goal. It was grueling work, and there were few signs of improvement for a long time. But by the summer of 1972 he was ready to work out with his team.

At first he played for short periods, and his old speed and agility were definitely not there. Gradually he performed better. That winter, when the Knicks won the 1973 National Basketball Association championship against the Los Angeles Lakers, Willis Reed played all the way through the season and the final series. He was selected as "most valuable player" by *Sport* magazine and was awarded the *Maurice Stokes Memorial Trophy* for the comeback of that year.

Willis Reed beat the odds because he had a goal he kept before his mind's eye and would not stop pursuing it.

3. Plan out the steps you will need to take to reach your goals.

Louis L'Amour, author of countless books of western lawmen, heroes, and bad guys, said, "People don't wear out; they give up. As far as trails go, there's always an open trail for the mind if you keep the doors open and give it a chance."[3]

The idea of different trails and open doors is a good one. Once you've worked out your goal, the next step is to break it all into pieces and steps. Where do I go from here? is literally the question. What process must I go through to get from A to B and then to C and D? It only makes sense to boil down a long-term goal into short-term efforts. That's the way it is with nearly everything in life. Nothing great happens instantaneously. Even a child needs eighteen or more years to grow up, and each stage has a multitude of required steps. On the missionary journeys, Paul moved to one city at a time. Jesus went from city to city and did not delay when others asked Him to. He had a plan; He knew where He was going. He took it step by step.

You must figure out how to accomplish your goal. My first thought was to work harder so I could earn extra money to pay the debts. I would get up early and go to bed late. Mary Alice would arrange ways for me to spend time with my daughters, despite my hectic schedule. They would join me for breakfast if I had to leave extremely early.

With my diabetes, the schedule was tough to keep, but I knew I couldn't give up. I fought back with my usual sit-ups every morning before I left the house, no matter how early. For me, deciding to exercise every day is a goal I made more than twenty-five years ago, and it's one I've kept. If I didn't exercise, I knew I would not live long. So any other goals I might have would be rendered meaningless.

As I thought about my financial problem with the buildings we had cosigned for, some other answers occurred to me. Two psychiatrists from Austin attended a seminar at our Dallas Clinic. I was impressed with them and asked them to join us. They were not willing to relocate, but they suggested that they open an Austin branch of our clinic. We investigated the possibility and agreed to terms. Then we moved them into the Austin building, which rented that space to capacity. Now we were no longer losing money as we paid the mortgage each month. And, as I mentioned in Chapter 3, Paul and I decided to use the Richardson building for a day hospital. That facility was soon ministering to hundreds of patients on a daily basis.

4. Accomplish one step and then reward yourself.

If you lose ten pounds, give yourself a present (but don't go out for pizza!). If you pay off part of a debt, celebrate with your spouse, family, or friends. When Thomas Edison marked some inventive milestone, he would treat himself to a slice of his wife's apple pie. (In fact, that was nearly all Edison ever ate, some say.)

Give yourself a break. Relax. Have a lemonade. Go out on the town. Take in a show. Reward yourself with something nice. You've accomplished something for yourself.

Once you've rewarded yourself for a job well done, go on to the other steps, with rewards at appropriate places. It's a relatively simple process but a proven one. The hard-working employee who gets rewarded by the boss is motivated to even more hard work. God Himself encourages us, "whatever you do, do it heartily, as to the Lord," knowing that "from the Lord you will receive the reward of the inheritance."[4]

5. Recognize what part is in your hands and what is in God's.

Solomon instructed us in Proverbs 16:3, "Commit your works to the LORD, / And your thoughts will be established." That is an important ingredient to bring into all your plans and hopes and dreams. Put God's part in His hands, then do *your* part. That means you can only commit plans that He will support. Such scrutiny and evaluation can change a person's whole direction, as it has with many Christians who have changed careers and even completely changed their lives in order to live up to God's truth in a difficult situation.

One young man I'll call Tom became a Christian and soon admitted his closet was full of clothing he'd shoplifted from a local store. He was in a tough spot, to say the least. After praying about this, he devised a plan of action. He would gather all the clothing together, take it back to the store, and ask for its value so he could pay the bill.

Could he make restitution and not go to jail? Probably not. But he determined to do what he could—and let God do the rest.

Initially Tom went to the store's manager, who then directed him to security. The tough store guards listened to his story and incredibly decided to show leniency if he paid for the clothing at the going rate. When it was all paid off, the security guard said to him, "Yeah, we get people in here every once in a while who have some religious experience or somethin' and they want to get rid of their guilt. It's pretty common, really."

The odds this time were in Tom's own mind, and he almost wilted in the process. He argued with God in prayer several times about the plan. But in the end God prevailed, and Tom emerged a stronger and better Christian.

6. Expect God to inspire you with ideas.

In the midst of all your planning to overcome the odds, remember you're not alone. God will lead you. Expect Him to flood your mind with variations on the theme, with new ideas and methods that may not have occurred to you. When certain tools, methods, or books come to your attention seemingly out of the blue, they are gifts with which God intends to help you reach your desired goals.

In counseling, people often tell me that as they went about working through a problem some coincidence occurred that helped them considerably. Such coincidences are not circumstantial; they're God's way of leading and guiding us through the rough currents.

The belief that you are not alone, that an almighty

God is with you and guiding you, is a powerful resource to mental and spiritual health. Bruno Bettelheim, the well-known child psychologist, was a survivor of Hitler's extermination camps. He said, "It is a well-known fact of the concentration camps that those who had strong religious and moral convictions managed life there much better than the rest. Their beliefs, including belief in an afterlife, gave them a strength to endure which was far above that of most others."[5]

Remember the story of Peter praying on the housetop? The whole future of Christianity and Jesus' mission lay in the hands of one very prejudiced man who could not leave behind the Jewish dietary laws and the exclusion of Gentiles from Jewish worship and observance. But as he prayed, he suddenly fell into a trance and God revealed to him a remarkable picture of all kinds of four-footed animals, wild beasts, creeping things, and birds of the air. "And a voice came to him, 'Rise, Peter; kill and eat.'"[6] Some of these foods were kosher and some were forbidden. Yet God was telling him to eat, reminding him, "What God has cleansed you must not call common." Through this leading, Peter realized that Gentiles were no longer "unclean"; therefore he could not only preach to them and convert them, but he could also include them in the fellowship as genuine disciples of Christ.

In the same way, God led Philip to the Ethiopian

eunuch, and he led Paul to his first missionary journey. The point is that God leads. He may not lead us in the same way as in olden times—through visions or appearances of angels—but He still reserves the right to do so. Now He mostly leads us through Scripture, prayer, the counsel of other believers, inspiration, and simple common sense. As John Calvin said, "It is better to limp in the way than to run with swiftness out of it."

7. Evaluate, refine, try again.

Few activities reach the pinnacle of perfection the first time out. In fact, few ever reach that point at all. In fighting back against the odds, repeated evaluation and refinement are paramount. There's almost always a better, more efficient, more productive way.

That doesn't mean there's no place for tradition, and it doesn't mean that certain activities should be constantly scrutinized. My exercise routine has changed little over the years. It's one of those "old standbys" that I trust I'll do into my nineties.

On the other hand, in going up against the odds it's always necessary to retrench, rethink, and attack again. There will be times of defeat and failure. There may even be circumstances when a complete turnaround is called for.

I have heard that Dr. James Dobson began his speaking career with little effectiveness, but continual evaluation, correction, and redirection helped him become one of the foremost public speakers of our age. Even Arnold Schwarzenegger, who played little more than "goon" roles in his first appearances in the movies, is now a top box-office attraction because he worked at honing his craft. I also know teachers who evaluate every class they teach to learn what to keep in their lesson plan and what to change.

The results of evaluation are better performance, stronger persona, and more resilient self-esteem. Through evaluation, the odds are reduced dramatically simply because you're learning from your mistakes and moving on.

8. Refuse to give up except in the face of truth and honor or good sense.

Sometimes there are good reasons to cut and run or even to quit the battlefield. In fact some military commanders say the secret of victory is knowing when to cut your losses.

Likewise, in the spiritual realm, there are times to reconsider whether what you're trying to do is possible and/or probable. But at the same time, a refusal to give in is far more necessary.

Harriet Beecher Stowe, who promoted the end of slavery in America through her book, *Uncle Tom's Cabin,* said, "When you get into a tight place and everything goes against you, till it seems as though you could not hold on a minute longer, never give up then, for that is just the place and time that the tide will turn."

Calvin Coolidge brought in another angle: "Nothing in the world can take the place of persistence. Talent will not; nothing is more common than unsuccessful men with talent. Genius will not; unrewarded genius is almost a proverb. Education will not; the world is full of educated derelicts. Persistence and determination alone are omnipotent."

I'm not sure I'd call them omnipotent, but clearly persistence and determination do pay. And yet, how few people are really willing to be anything close to persistent and determined! There's a price tag on those qualities. It seems as if they are characteristics you either have or you don't have. But that's simply not true; they are qualities that you *choose* to have. They are components of will.

Eventually I paid off the notes on those two buildings. God blessed me. I acted with integrity, I was strong physically, and Mary Alice, the girls, and I had never been closer. Oh, yes, Mary Alice also talked with the banker. "Any words of advice?" she asked.

"Yes, put your husband's hands in concrete so he can't sign any more notes," he said.

Never again did I sign any bank notes. Those two years of my life read like the six o'clock news, a real Hollywood nightmare!

Anyone can be persistent if he or she believes in something. It's those who believe in nothing, or at least don't believe strongly enough to act, who never see success in any form. Those who truly believe change the world. (Unfortunately, that even works for erroneous beliefs at times!)

Well-known artist Norman Rockwell built his success on perseverance and hard work. He made his first sale of two magazine covers to George Horace Lorimer, editor of the *Saturday Evening Post,* for seventy-five dollars apiece in March 1916 and could not have been happier. He hurried to his boarding-house and boasted to a young schoolteacher living there (with whom he was in love), "I will never paint again for children's magazines." He believed he had truly arrived, so he asked the girl to marry him! She refused at first, then accepted later!

Rockwell went to work on the third cover he'd contracted for the *Post,* an illustration of an old man playing baseball with a group of kids. He completed some drafts and took them to Philadelphia to show to George Lorimer.

This time there were problems. Lorimer felt the old man was a bit rough, even hobolike. He asked the artist to do it over.

Rockwell went home and redid the portrait. Again, the editor told Norman the man was still too old, so he repainted it again. The next time the boy was too small. Rockwell decided that working for the *Post* was much more formidable than he'd supposed, but he painted yet another version. Rockwell redid that painting five times before Lorimer was satisfied and forked over the next payment! Later Lorimer told Norman Rockwell he'd merely been testing him. Norman refrained from telling him how close he'd come to quitting!

It's that kind of persistence that pays, that beats the odds.

I have to say one more thing: *Dream on.* Beating the odds is the stuff of dreams. We dream about overcoming a problem at work, a difficulty in the home, or an overwhelming and distressing shame in our lives. They are all beatable—with persistence, perseverance, determination, and a little panache thrown in.

Many years ago the statesman and great orator Winston Churchill was asked to speak at Harvard's commencement. He approached the platform and said, "Never give up, never give up, never give up, never give up, never give up, never give up, never give up, never give up." He then sat down.

Winston Churchill knew what he was talking about. He led England through the Second World War. He walked London's streets after Hitler's air force had battered parts of that great city into rubble.

Undoubtedly, Winston Churchill was not the brand of religious fanatic that I am, but he did prove the principle I'm writing about. In fact, if his life was anything, the drone of the words, *I can because I believe I can,* was what made him what he was. He was a bulldog because he was convinced he was right, the job could be done, and in the end it could be won. If he hadn't had such conviction, he could never have aroused England during the onslaught of Hitler's military typhoon.

Every now and then I take a look at his words to the English people during that time:

"We shall not flag or fail. We shall go on to the end. We shall fight in France, we shall fight on the seas and oceans, we shall fight . . . in the air. We shall defend our island, whatever the cost may be. We shall fight on the beaches, we shall fight on the landing grounds, we shall fight in the fields and in the streets, we shall fight in the hills; we shall never surrender. And even if, which I do not for a moment believe, this island . . . were subjugated and starving, then our empire beyond the seas, armed and guarded by the British Fleet, would carry on the struggle, until, in God's good time, the new world, with all its power and might, steps forth to the rescue and the liberation of the old."

Life, he believed, could be summarized in just three words: Never give up.

CHAPTER 7

The Ultimate Victory

 *Grow Through Defeat*

Overcoming the odds has been such a passion for me, sometimes I go too far. Mary Alice certainly thought so one day when she saw the month-old wolf cub I had ordered through the mail. "Frank, you have really done it this time! You've gone off the deep end," she probably wanted to say.

I knew she was shocked, but I also noted a twinkle in her eye and a smile twitching at the edge of her lips as she picked up the little cub. Of all people, Mary Alice has grown accustomed to my relentless pursuit of going against the odds.

The cub was from North Carolina, but her grandparents had come from McKinsey Valley in Canada.

"We'll name her Miss McKinsey," I said as my daughters ran in and we all played with our newfound friend. I had taken the summer off to spend with Mary Alice and the girls after a harrowing year of long hours and hard work in the hospital. Many mornings I had arisen at 3:00 A.M. to start my day's work. The thought of a summer in a remote mountain-wilderness retreat with my loved ones seemed almost too good to be true. But here we were and it was all just starting—with the arrival of my latest attempt to do something different.

Miss McKinsey was born out of two of the largest wolf parents in captivity (her father weighed 170 pounds, and her mother weighed 116). The parents' coloring had been typical gray and white. Yet, when Miss McKinsey arrived she was a whitish golden color similar to that of a golden palomino.

I had never seen a wolf with such odd coloring before. In every other sense—the sharp eyes, long nose, gleaming teeth, and V-shaped wolf head—she looked like a typical wolf, at least to me. Miss McKinsey began to grow into a beautiful large golden vision of raw but tamed power.

Miss McKinsey soon recognized her new name, coming when called and even learning a few tricks. I had always heard that wolves are very pack oriented. And the way she seemed to love all of us, I guess she felt she had found her pack.

That summer did not disappoint us. We went horseback riding with Miss McKinsey trotting and galloping along behind us, yapping to her heart's content. When we swam in the crystal-clear, old-time swimming hole at a juncture in the local stream, Miss McKinsey plowed in with us. As we sprinted through the fields and woods, she dashed along next to us, full of fun and mischief and a bent for comedy. As a family, we all grew close in ways I had missed. Miss McKinsey, our wolf cub turned family pet, was always nearby, becoming more and more a part of our little family.

Miss McKinsey never did seem to understand that by legend wolves are supposed to be mean and fierce. Though we were all a little nervous about it, she never showed a mean bone in her body. In fact, she was exceptionally friendly with everyone, even with other animals. That summer, she and a fawn took up with each other, playing and gamboling around on the grass. I would watch in amazement as they would rub noses. "What an odd wolf," I said to Mary Alice more than once. Then I would have to explain, with my little note of triumph—thinking she was a bit like me—"She's going against the odds."

One winter I decided it was time to send Miss McKinsey to retriever training school. Mary Alice didn't like the idea so much. "Frank, wolves aren't retrievers; it is not in their genes," she told me.

"I know," I said, and I guess that little knot of desire to do something different struck again because I added, "I love beating the odds. Let's give it a shot."

By early next spring the trainer was taking the

golden wolf (which, he always told admirers, belonged to "the crazy psychiatrist in Dallas") to all of the Labrador retriever contests. She was not allowed to compete, but the trainer enjoyed showing all of his friends how he had taught a wolf to retrieve even better than many of their Labs. I was not surprised, for I had heard that the brain of a wolf is considerably larger than that of a dog, and I knew Miss McKinsey was far smarter than any dog I had ever had. Mary Alice, this time finessing me with my favorite line, said, "Well, she beats the odds again."

I guess I've been sounding a little prideful about all this, going on about how nice Miss McKinsey was and how she always went against the odds. There was a time, however, when I thought the whole process of raising Miss McKinsey was leading to sure defeat.

It was the Fourth of July. Alicia had just been born, and Mary Alice was still in the hospital. Grandmother was visiting. A friend, Brian Spencer, had come over, and I was grilling hamburgers. Everyone was ecstatic. Rachel, Renee, and Carrie had a new baby sister. Even the animals on the ranch seemed happy.

Then it happened. "Daddy, Daddy," Renee screamed, "come quick! Miss McKinsey has attacked Betsy and Wilbur!" Betsy was our six-hundred-pound hog; Wilbur was our little Vietnamese pot-bellied pig. (By now you realize how much we all like pets!) "Oh, Daddy," Renee continued, "you know how I always used to love to curl my finger through Betsy's tail—well, her tail's now on the wall! And Wilbur's cute little ears—well, they're on the floor! Blood is everywhere—on the floor, on the walls. Come quickly, Daddy! Do something."

I ran out to the barn and found Miss McKinsey in the middle of a huge brouhaha. Grabbing her by the collar, I yelled, "Miss McKinsey, what have you done? Shame on you! You know better than that."

The big golden wolf hung her head. However, Betsy and Wilbur, now tail-less and ear-less, did not seem to be impressed with her repentance. Indeed, their blood was all over the place.

I hurriedly called the veterinarian. "All right, don't worry," he said. "Just bring Betsy and Wilbur in."

"I can't bring in a six-hundred-pound hog!" I said.

"Oh! That's right," he answered. "I'll be right out."

Never again did Miss McKinsey disappoint me. She truly always seemed devastated when she saw my disapproval. From then on she seemed to understand my desire that she beat the odds—and prove it to everyone else!

As our friend Brian finished burning, I mean frying, the hamburgers, Renee shared all the gory details with Mary Alice by phone. Soon everyone recovered, and no one even had to go through psy-chotherapy! Oh, yes, Betsy and Wilbur did fine, too—Betsy's tail remained affixed, and Wilbur's ears were soon back in shape.

I have grown wiser today, and I would certainly advise against having a wolf or a wolf dog as a pet, but I must be honest and say that indeed Miss McKinsey did bring a lot of joy, fun, and encour-agement into our lives. She went against the odds. She and I both grew through defeat. Miss McKinsey learned when she lost and as a result she didn't lose again. Her story is a humorous one, borne out of my desire to beat the odds; other failures and defeats in my life—and in yours—have been more serious.

THE COMMONALITY OF DEFEAT

Defeat, failure, setbacks, and all-out destruction are things many Christians never get used to. They wonder, *Why did God do this to me?* Or they ask, "Why did this have to happen?" And they blame God, feeling that somehow He has given them a raw deal in life.

Yet I have learned some things about defeat and failure as a Christian, the primary one being that you can learn and grow through defeat so you can eventually overcome the odds and not be defeated in that area again.

William G. Milnes, Jr., wrote in *The Saturday Evening Post,* "You're on the road to success when you realize that failure is merely a detour."

THE BIBLE ON DEFEAT

The Bible is full of admonitions about success and failure, trouble, problems, and persecution. Consider a few of these famous words from the apostle Paul, who was very familiar with defeat:

"And not only that, but we also glory in tribulations, knowing that tribulation produces perseverance; and perseverance, character; and character, hope. Now hope does not disappoint, because the love of God has been poured out in our hearts by the Holy Spirit who was given to us."[1]

And later in Romans 8:18 Paul said, "For I consider that the sufferings of this present time are not worthy to be compared with the glory which shall be revealed in us."

Paul told the Philippians, who, from the tone of the book, were frightened and defeated by Paul's imprisonment, "I want you to know, brethren, that the things which happened to me have actually turned out for the furtherance of the gospel, so that it has become evident to the whole palace guard, and to all the rest, that my chains are in Christ; and most of the brethren in the Lord, having become confident by my chains, are much more bold to speak the word without fear."[2]

In fact, Paul suffered from constant defeat as witnessed by his writings, and yet he kept a continually upbeat attitude.

The whole book of Revelation was written to saints in the worst state of defeat and trouble. Yet, the book ends with Jesus' uplifting word of hope, "Surely I am coming quickly."

Learning to deal with failure is important, not only from a psychological and spiritual point of view, but also from a practical standpoint. J. Wallace Hamilton was quoted in *Leadership Magazine* on the subject of failure and defeat. He said, "The increase of suicides, alcoholics, and even some forms of nervous breakdowns is evidence that many people are training for success when they should be training for failure. Failure is far more common than success; poverty is more prevalent than wealth, and disappointment more normal than arrival."

Think of some of the great failures of biblical history: Adam and Eve, who received God's first great promise of a Savior and yet gave in to the devil's temptation. Noah, whose pain after the flood was so great he got drunk, and yet he went on to claim his place in history. Abraham, who lied his way out of bad situations twice (only to make them worse) and yet was God's first great man of faith. Moses, who at forty was a vagrant in the wilderness and spent the next forty years in seething obscurity and yet became Israel's greatest leader. David, who after a series of stunning successes failed miserably by committing adultery and murder and yet was called "the man after God's own heart." Jonah, whose attempt at suicide was stopped by being swallowed by a great fish, and yet he went on to cause the greatest revival in history.

In the New Testament, we have the continually bumbling, babbling disciples, who set the world on fire and wrote the New Testament—and after whom we name our children. Even Jesus, at one point, looked like the world's greatest fool, but resurrection turned Him into the world's Savior and King.

Throughout history we see other colossal failures: Savonarola, the monk who preached in Florence, Italy, met failure at every turn but later became Italy's greatest orator. Martin Luther, a man of temper and beer drinking, set the Protestant Reformation in motion. Daniel Webster, one of America's greatest politicians and speakers, could not make an effective speech until he'd spent years of effort. George Washington lost more battles than he won.

Indeed, people today need to know more about how to work on in spite of setbacks, failure, and defeat than they do about success because success always seems to be stationed at the end of the line.

HOW TO GROW IN THE FACE OF DEFEAT

How, then, should we respond to defeat? Let me offer six biblically based principles that are both practical and helpful.

1. Recognize that defeat happens because we're in a war, one that we will ultimately win.

Paul wrote in Ephesians 6:12, "We do not wrestle against flesh and blood, but against principalities, against powers, against the rulers of the darkness of this age, against spiritual hosts of wickedness in the heavenly places."

There is a war going on around us, an invisible war that rages every moment of the day. Satan and his hordes have one objective: to derail the ultimate plan of God. They don't care how this is accomplished. They will throw up any roadblock, any negative thought, any evil idea that will get them to that place.

I often see a mentality in Christian circles that implies, Now that we're Christians, we should succeed. The odds should go down. Life should become easier. We should not suffer failure and defeat.

But just the reverse is true. Becoming a Christian will invite more problems, more opposition, more activity in the spiritual realm *against* us! Anytime we seek to glorify God, Satan's going to focus on us very fast. He'll send in a whole committee of demons to oppose us if one demon can't do it. He doesn't care about all the non-Christians out there who care nothing for Christ. They'll do fine without demonic influence. It's the determined, hard-driving Christian that Satan will oppose every step of the way.

Of course, that doesn't mean we face certain defeat. As I tried to show in Chapter 5, God is with us. He limits Satan's power and activity. He throws up a hedge around us as He did with Job so that Satan is literally stymied in his efforts to fell us. Yet there are times He gives Satan more room to maneuver and "work us over." Satan asked to attack Job, and God allowed him to do so. Satan asked that God give him the opportunity to sift Peter like wheat. And Jesus said, "Okay." Jesus Himself was led up by the Spirit to be tempted in the wilderness.

I believe we must assume that Satan and his cohorts are always petitioning God's throne to be allowed to "sift us." Certainly, most of the time God only gives him highly limited freedom in that area, but at other times, God tests us. He allows us to go through difficulties and problems that would even stagger angels. Yet, all the time He is there with us through every battle, through every problem. He never forsakes us or deserts us. Never!

When you realize that defeat is the result of being engaged in battle, your perspective changes. You see that you're doing something for God. When you go down to defeat because Satan has opposed you, there's a certain sense in which you should be emboldened, believing, "If Satan is fighting me this hard, I must be doing something important!"

The amazing thing about the apostle Paul is that he kept going. When I read the list of problems he faced in 2 Corinthians 11, I'm astonished that he didn't give up. There were beatings with rods and the lash. He was stoned once and died, some interpreters believe, only to revive and face other hardships. He was shipwrecked, and he found himself opposed by the Jews and Romans everywhere he went. Ultimately, he was beheaded. But was his life a success? Certainly. Why? Because he expected to be opposed, so opposition never stopped him.

Woodrow Wilson said, "I would rather fail in a cause that will one day succeed than succeed in a cause that will one day fail." That was Paul. Piled-up failures and defeats didn't stop him because he knew that would happen from the beginning. Listen to what he told the Thessalonians: "[We] sent Timothy, our brother and minister of God, and our fellow laborer in the gospel of Christ, to establish you and encourage you concerning your faith, that no one should be shaken by these afflictions; for you yourselves know that we are appointed to this.

For, in fact, we told you before when we were with you that we would suffer tribulation, just as it happened, and you know."[3] Obviously, Paul knew what he was in for when he embarked on his mission.

Paul expected problems, not because he was a masochist, not because he liked them, but because he knew he was in the middle of a war. He was on the battlefield, and what happens on battlefields? Battle! Strife! Anger! Difficulties! Persecution! Opposition! Fighting to the death!

I remind you of this principle because it's important to realize that you will suffer defeat at times as part of your battle with the devil, the world, and the flesh. These are powerful forces that want to destroy each of us. Their goal is our heads on Satan's platter!

2. See defeat as an opportunity to rely on God for victory.

Yet defeat is an opportunity to rely on God. It tells us, in essence, "Here's another reason to rely on and consult and be supported by the power of the Spirit." After all, Jesus said, "Without Me you can do nothing."[4] Sometimes we have to ask, Am I being defeated because God is showing me that I'm not relying on Him?

When Paul was stoned and beaten with rods, he must have been severely hurt. Yet somehow he got up and went on. How? Because he ran right back to the Lord in his heart and mind and asked for help.

I remember hearing about a little boy whose father asked him to remove a rock from the backyard. The boy went out and tried to lift it but he couldn't. Soon he gave up. His father said, "Have you tried everything?" The boy replied, "Yes." The father countered, "No, you haven't. You haven't asked me to help you. Together we can do the job."

So many Christians look at defeat as a final thing when God means it to force us to come running back to Him for strength and thereby grow in our relationship with Him. As Jesus faced greater pharisaical opposition bent on stopping Him, he continued on, spreading His message, teaching, and encouraging His followers. How was He able to do that? Because He spent time in prayer each morning and relied on His Father to give Him strength.

I think of Joni Eareckson Tada, whose radio program, *Joni and Friends,* is aired right after *The Minirth Meier New Life Clinic Program* on some stations. Anyone who has read her classic story, *Joni,* understands the struggle she went through after her paralyzing accident that left her a quadriplegic at the age of seventeen. Prior to the accident, Joni had dreamed of riding horses in equestrian events, possibly even the Olympics, and she had been a vigorous swimmer. She had loved dating, parties, artwork, and all the activities of a typical teenager.

That accident derailed everything. She could not feed herself. She could not perform the most normal, intimate things such as brushing her teeth, using the bathroom, putting on makeup, or lifting a cup of water to her lips. For more than two years, she struggled with deep depression.

But eventually, through the help of various mentors, friends, family members, and counselors, she found a way out of the darkness. The first biblical principle she practiced is found in 1 Thessalonians 5:18: "In everything give thanks; for this is the will of God in Christ Jesus for you." She could not see how her situation was a reason for gratitude, but Steve Estes, a good friend and ardent theological student, assured her it was. Finally, she gave thanks, and her life was transformed. Something changed in that moment.

Joni decided that whatever Christ would enable her to do, she would do. She would see the accident as an opportunity to rely on God for victory. If He was with her, she could do many things she previously thought impossible. One of them came out in the area of art. Joni found by putting a felt-tip pen in her teeth she could draw—not just squiggly lines, but pieces of art any artist would be proud to exhibit. And indeed many of her portraits are available today on greeting cards, in gift shops, and as framed paintings and etchings.

As news of her abilities spread, she was invited to

talk on television and various talk shows. She learned to speak gospel messages in public—even though it was something she had been terrified of for years—and became an inspiring, heart-touching spokeswoman for Christ.

As she learned to do these things, she found that sometimes she liked to stop and sing a new song as she spoke to crowds, just to encourage them and lift their hearts. What happened? Soon a record company approached her about recording an album.

Next, *Joni and Friends* was launched. Joni's radio program now is featured all over the world, encouraging handicapped people and their friends to rely on God so He can work their circumstances for good.

What if Joni had decided she simply couldn't take that first step? Would any amount of Scripture, promises, teaching, and training have put her where she is today? In reality, Joni would be the first to tell us that any good she has done has only been because she relied on God. But there are multitudes of handicapped Christians in similar situations. Some have profited from her counsel and gone on to effective ministries and happy lives, but it's only because they have taken God at His Word and believed that His promise is true: "I am with you always." They have relied on Him.

So many times I counsel people who don't turn to God until literally all is lost. That's not the time to

do it. The time to turn to the Lord is at that first sign
of trouble. He promises to lead us through it.

Jimmy Carter, whose tenure as president many
consider a rank failure, has gone on to help the
homeless, negotiate settlements in wartorn nations,
and found a number of organizations dedicated to
peace. *Time* magazine called him our "best ex-
President because of all the things he's done out of
office."

Those who go back to their roots, rekindle their
faith, and come back swinging with the belief that
God is on their side are the ones who win both
human and divine admiration.

3. See defeat as part of a process God is taking you through.

The Spirit of God is perfecting us, making us like
Jesus. And part of the way He does that is through
defeat and failure. He promises, "that He who has
begun a good work in you will complete it until the
day of Jesus Christ."[5] How did God do that with
Moses? By letting him suffer defeats and setbacks.
As he endured each one Moses learned something
new. He came back, saw that God was with him and
that the defeat wasn't permanent, and he kept on
going.

In this respect we must be careful not to spend
too much time bemoaning our defeats. If they're
part of the process God is using to perfect us, then

they are good for us in some sense, a medicine we must take to ultimately be made whole.

An unforgettable story from Abigail Van Buren's syndicated "Dear Abby" column concerns that very issue. The writer tells of how a high school English class arrived at school to find a bottle of milk inside a stone crock, sitting on the teacher's desk. "I'm going to teach you something this morning that has nothing to do with teaching English but everything to do with life," she said. She then picked up the bottle and dashed it against the inside of the stone crock.

"The lesson is," the teacher said, "don't cry over spilled milk." She had everyone come up and look at the broken bits of glass mixed with milk in the bottom of the crock.

"I want all of you to remember this. Would any of you attempt to restore the bottle to its original form? Does it do any good to wish the bottle had not been broken? Look at this mess! You can moan about it forever, but it won't put the bottle back together again. Remember this broken bottle of milk when something happens in your life that nothing can undo."[6]

When you see defeat as part of the process of growth, you can interpret a negative event as a positive force in your life. After all, what is more desirable: to win in this life and lose in heaven, or to experience all that God sends us—even defeats—

and then in faith pluck on, knowing that one day He will say to us, "Well done!"?

God works in many ways in our world, and a primary way is through suffering, problems, difficulties, and defeats.

I have read of a man who was born in 1879 to a poor Jewish merchant. Because of the anti-Jewish attitude he encountered in his homeland, he suffered from a harrowing sense of inferiority much of his life. He learned slowly and was shy, introspective to a fault. His parents even had him examined by a specialist to see if he was normal. In 1895 he was not admitted to the Polytechnicum school in Zurich, Switzerland, because he failed the entrance exams. A year later, he tried again and was received. Years later, he was awarded a doctorate at the University of Zurich and obtained a job as a patent examiner in a Bern office. During that time he tinkered with the ideas he had about the universe and his world. Eventually he came up with a theory to explain how time, space, gravitation, and the worlds worked. He called it the Theory of Relativity. His name was Albert Einstein.

We psychiatrists often see people who are filled with guilt, regret, and grief because of the problems they've had or the failures they've endured. Don't bemoan defeat, but see it as a part of the process God is taking you through to make you a stronger, more resilient, and more effective Christian.

4. Use defeat to learn about life and yourself.

The old maxim, If at first you don't succeed, try, try again, could be better phrased, If at first you don't succeed, analyze the reasons for your defeat, and then try, try again. Science is, in fact, a process of trial and error. An employee of Minnesota Mining and Manufacturing, the 3-M Corporation, was trying to find a new kind of glue. He just happened upon a glue that would stick, but not so tight that it could not be removed or left a residue. Unknowingly, he had invented the little yellow "Post-It" notes so popular today.

Assess the situation. Take a hard look at what went wrong. Study the opposition just as a football coach and his team watch the movies of the opposing teams to learn their weaknesses. William Bolitho said, "The most important thing in life is not to capitalize on your gains. Any fool can do that. The really important thing is to profit from your losses. That requires intelligence; and it makes the difference between a man of sense and a fool."

In 1860 a thirty-eight-year-old man worked as a handyman for his dad, a leather merchant. The son kept the books, drove wagons, and checked hides for a salary of sixty-six dollars a month. Before this job, the man had failed as a soldier, a farmer, and a real estate agent. Many people who knew him had written him off as a complete failure.

Eight years later he was president of the United States. His name was Ulysses S. Grant.

When Grant went into a battle during the Civil War, he constantly calculated how he could beat the odds. He worked at getting better intelligence, better equipment, better men in the battle—all to reduce the odds against him. And those odds were great. At the beginning of the war, the South had the better generals and a far more committed army. Even to the end, they were a powerful fighting force. They were beaten by attrition and superior leadership—after Grant came into the picture. Grant had used his previous failures to learn about life and about himself. He used that knowledge to lead the Northern armies to victory.

5. Are you trying to go it alone? Analyze defeat from a team perspective.

Without all my coworkers, partners, and friends in the Minirth Meier New Life Clinic, I know we would never accomplish what we have. It's not my efforts that give us success; it's the team's efforts. Few of us can succeed in any venture alone. Lincoln had his Grant and Meade and Hooker as well as hundreds of thousands of others. Washington had Jefferson, Franklin, and Paine along with the whole Revolutionary War council and army. Even Edison had a group of researchers and experimenters helping him, including his well-known associate Dr. Carl Steinmetz.

Few efforts in life are a single achievement. True, the awards may come to one person, but he or she ultimately must recognize all those who helped him get there, including Mom and Dad, friends, relatives, and others.

Many business leaders say the test of a great manager is who he hires. Getting the right people to join your team is paramount.

John Sculley, former president and CEO of Apple Corporation, was approached years ago by Stephen Jobs, the founder of Apple. The company was floundering, and they needed a solid executive to get them back on course. When Jobs approached Sculley, the latter was already a successful executive with Pepsi-Cola. After some discussion about the position, Sculley turned down Jobs's offer. He could not leave his home and uproot his family to go to California. Jobs asked what he had to pay him to get him to come. Sculley replied that he'd need a million dollars a year, a million to sign, and a million bonus. Jobs thought about it, then made that offer. John Sculley still balked.

Then Stephen Jobs hit him with the final question: "Do you want to sell sugar water for the rest of your life, or do you want to change the world?"

That did it! Sculley went with Apple, and the rest is history. Sculley turned Apple Corporation around with his management skills and made it the powerful computer company that it is today.

Maybe what God is teaching you when He allows you to be defeated is this: Don't go it alone. Don't try to do everything yourself. That's a sure path to burnout and frustration. So ask yourself, "Who do I need at my side to change this situation? Who can I trust to reverse this loss?"

Those are the kinds of questions Paul Meier and I asked when we put our team together. We looked for good people, honest people, the right people— and once we found them, we gave them what they needed to get the job done. We're still doing that today because people are always leaving and changing careers. It's the greatest test of management and success. Few can go it alone.

Think of what Jesus had to do in choosing those first twelve men (one of whom He knew would betray Him). He prayed the whole night before selecting His team. He depended upon His Father to guide Him. He looked for people in whom He saw that spark of life and commitment. And then He called them. (We don't read of Him calling others.) He didn't try to go it alone.

6. What looks like sure defeat can be turned by God into something good.

For the Christian, one truth supersedes everything that happens in our lives: Romans 8:28—"We know that all things work together for good to those who love God, to those who are the called accord-

SEVEN PRINCIPLES FOR OVERCOMING THE ODDS

ing to His purpose." Paul saw that happen again and again in his life. For every step back there were two steps forward. He learned to see that the steps back were God's way of redirecting his efforts. When God allowed him to be wounded with a thorn in the flesh and he appealed to God to take it away, God told him, "My strength is made perfect in weakness." What was Paul's response? To complain? To become bitter? To challenge God's wisdom and accuse Him of shortchanging him on life?

No. Paul wrote, "Most gladly I will rather boast in my infirmities, that the power of Christ may rest upon me. Therefore I take pleasure in infirmities, in reproaches, in needs, in persecutions, in distresses, for Christ's sake. For when I am weak, then I am strong."[7]

That's a tremendously difficult attitude to attain, especially in our world that is so intent on blaming someone else for all the things that happen to us. But it's not impossible.

There is a great old story about the pianist Jan Paderewski of Poland who was giving a recital. Before he came on, a fidgety boy clambered up onto the platform and, to the horror of the crowd, began playing an unpracticed version of "Chopsticks." Hundreds of faces turned and frowned at the sight; then some shouted, "Get that boy away from here! Somebody stop him!"

Backstage, Paderewski heard the commotion,

pulled on his coat, and rushed out. Without a word, he bent over the boy and flowed around him with beautiful, improvised music. As the boy looked up, Paderewski just whispered, "Keep playing, son. Don't quit. Keep on playing."

When they finished there was thunderous applause.

That is, in essence, what God promises to do with our failures, errors, and distresses. He'll play around them till they sound even better, and when we sit down in heaven, there will be thunderous applause!

CHAPTER 8

The Eternal Perspective

7 *See Life from God's Viewpoint*

I've had to fight hard all my life just to accomplish many ordinary things—medical school, starting practice, earning a seminary degree, passing state boards in neurology and psychiatry—because of the physical limitations of my diabetes. And when we moved to Dallas new challenges met me. I had come from rural Arkansas and was not used to the sophisticated lifestyle. I was like a fish out of water and a fish swimming upstream at that—against the odds. But by the mid-1980s I felt I had survived. I was traveling around America giving lectures on beating the odds—and I believed I truly had beaten the odds myself. And then all of a sudden I felt as if I was being abandoned by those closest to me.

One day a friend and clinic associate called to tell me, "I will be leaving the clinic soon. I believe I've got my priorities all backward. I want to stop to enjoy nature, life, and especially my family."

I understood, but it was disconcerting. He would be hard to replace.

Not too long after that I received another call. "I'm moving to California," my good friend and associate Paul Meier said.

"Let me guess. You want more time to enjoy nature, life, and your family," I replied. The pace of our clinics, with twenty offices throughout the United States, a radio show, and a multitude of new books, had drained him.

I tried to understand again, but I knew that another loss of a valuable person would put an even greater strain on the clinic.

Soon a third call came. After a brief salutation, another close friend and a counselor at our clinic said, "I'm moving to Austin."

"Don't tell me," I replied. "You want more time to enjoy nature, life, and the family, and I bet you long for the big, tall, stately oak trees." He wondered how I knew. We parted friends, but I was beginning to feel as if someone out there had my number. I would miss these key people and their contribution to the clinic.

Believe it or not a couple of months later a fourth call came. "I'm moving to Missouri," another associate said. "I love nature, life, family, and yes, trees."

Four of my best friends were traipsing off to places unknown and I would not have their support and friendship. And their support was crucial to me because I consider our team members essential to the clinic's success, as I've already mentioned. The loss of each of these persons individually would weaken the team; I feared the loss of four key people in such a short time could be devastating.

You may have experienced the same kind of situation in your workplace or on a volunteer committee where the most important players suddenly quit.

If I hadn't been able to see what was happening from God's perspective—that these changes must be part of His plan for these people and for me—I would have been extremely depressed.

For the Christian, life is not about piling up wealth, experiencing pleasures, reaching for fame, or building a great reputation that leads to prestige. Life is living for Jesus, knowing Him and walking with Him. That's the eternal perspective. If your perspective is anything less than that, I suspect you will ultimately be defeated and stymied in life. You will wonder at times if it's worth all the trouble. You will live the life of "quiet desperation" that Thoreau spoke about in *Walden* many years ago.

In the days after those fateful phone calls I read my Bible again and again to find guidance. The Scriptures that were meaningful to me all pointed to this eternal perspective and four truths that support it:

1. Nothing is lost. Nothing you do for God is in vain.

First, realize that God knows and holds everything in His hand. He has recorded it all in His book and nothing is lost. Nothing in life that we do for Him is forgotten or worthless or in vain. It will all ultimately be remembered and rewarded. A favorite verse of mine is 1 Corinthians 15:58: "Be steadfast, immovable, always abounding in the work of the Lord, knowing that your labor is not in vain in the Lord."

How many Christians have felt that their efforts are useless, believing, "We're not going to accomplish anything, so why try?" They look at their tiny Sunday school class and compare it to the hugeness of the world and think, "What good will any of this do?" I'm particularly discouraged when I look at the news and see the way the press reports the abortion issue. Conservative Christians are called "right-wingers," and "fanatics." The pro-abortion factions, though, are described as being "middle-of-the-roaders," and having a "wide-ranging coalition of support within the church and society at large." Sometimes newspaper headlines make us feel that our government is set against Christian values, and we despair of ever changing anything for good.

What was the apostle Paul's counsel in 1 Corinthians? "Be steadfast." Don't let yourself be shaken from your conviction. No matter who pooh-poohs your work, no matter what the neighbors say about "those nuts next door," keep on keeping on.

Why? Because God knows about it and He cares and He has said that if it glorifies Him, it's worthwhile. Remember what 1 Corinthians 15:58 says: "Your labor is not in vain in the Lord."

Whatever your work may be, whatever service you perform in the kingdom of God, your toil is not in vain! God does not measure things in sheer numbers the way we do. With three hundred dedicated men led by Gideon, God destroyed 120,000 Midianites. Through a lad of sixteen or so, God killed Goliath and then used that same David to conquer much of the Middle Eastern world. A youthful carpenter, Jesus, died for the sins of the world and still makes it possible for anyone anywhere to have eternal life.

The power of one is a classic truth. As the saying goes, "God plus one is a majority." Through one inflamed apostle named Paul, God turned the world upside down and started Christianity on the crest of a wave that is still rolling today. Through eleven other scared men, Jesus sent out emissaries to all parts of the known world and multitudes were converted. God does not need numbers to accomplish great ends. He just needs one or two. You and me!

So many of us don't recognize that even the little things we do now count for eternity. Being patient in a traffic jam is noticed by God. Giving that extra money to God's work when we could have chosen to use it to purchase a new VCR gets top billing in heaven. A child's giving up the bigger piece of cake to a little sister at dessert because he or she loves Jesus is remembered! God notices everything. He remembers everything. Nothing we do is ultimately meaningless. That outlook can only come from an eternal perspective, which sees us living with Jesus forever. Only when we realize that one day we will be with Him, and He will review all that we did in life, can we begin now to live each day with the verve and conviction that wins His approval.

Recognize that no deed you have done in righteousness will be overlooked. Maybe no one noticed it at the time. Maybe you didn't get an award in the here and now. Maybe the deed was misunderstood or people condemned you for doing it, but God sees it as gold and He will ultimately praise you for it!

2. We are assured of a reward.

Some argue that the idea of God rewarding us for deeds well done is crass and foolish. I don't agree because nearly every motivation in life is based on reward. We work and try to climb the ladder of success in order to gain a reward. We keep our homes neat in order to gain the reward of personal satisfaction, if not a compliment from our spouses. We get our children into Little League and Boy Scouts and Pioneer Girls, and they compete for rewards. So why should it seem so far-fetched that God extends to us the promise of rewards for our "deeds in the body"?

Like it or not, that's the truth. As Paul said in 2 Corinthians 5:10: "For we must all appear before the judgment seat of Christ, that each one may receive the things done in the body, according to what he has done, whether good or bad." What could be plainer or easier to understand?

Part of keeping an eternal perspective is knowing that God not only remembers our good deeds but that He will also reward us for them. This has nothing to do with salvation. We are saved by grace through faith. Nothing we have done—no lifelong service as a missionary or pastor, no commitment to the Heart Fund or MS research—can save us. Salvation can only come to those who believe in Christ and receive Him into their hearts. It's a free gift.

But the Bible says we will also be rewarded for our good deeds on earth. Paul says in Romans 2:6 that God "will render to each one according to his deeds." It's a basic principle of the Bible. What you sow, you reap. What you have done in this life will receive some kind of reward (or, if you never believed in God or Christ, a punishment).

I don't know about you, but that motivates me. Paul told the Colossians to work heartily "as to the Lord and not to men, knowing that from the Lord you will receive the reward of the inheritance."[1] Anything I have done for the Lord will be repaid to me in eternity, no matter what I get paid for my work in this life. Jesus made that clear when He told His disciples that "Whoever gives one of these little ones only a cup of cold water in the name of a disciple, assuredly, I say to you, he shall by no means lose his reward."[2]

If Jesus didn't mean some kind of real reward, whatever it might be, then why would He say such a thing?

The idea of rewards in heaven should motivate us—not to compete with one another, but to serve the Lord with all the more fortitude, knowing that no matter how poorly we are paid in this world, He will repay us in the next.

Henry C. Morrison, a missionary to Africa, returned to America by ship after forty years on the field. On the same ship was Theodore Roosevelt, returning from a hunting safari. At the docks, a huge crowd of well-wishers and the press turned out to greet the president and hunter. No one, though, had come to welcome Mr. Morrison. *I ought to get some recognition for the service I've performed all these years,* he thought, rather bitterly. But it looked like there was none.

Then a still small voice in his heart spoke, saying, "But Henry, you're not home yet."

When I think of how many Christians labor against the odds in lifelong obscurity—people who serve in businesses and give an honest day's work but will never even get a gold watch at the end of their service, missionaries who went to the field and lost nearly everything but stood the test and did the work without complaint—I realize how great this promise is. It means no one anywhere is insignificant. It means no one anywhere has a life that is worthless or useless. Everyone counts. Everything counts. It is all recorded, remembered, and will be rewarded. God assures all of us who are His, "You matter. Your life matters. What you do matters. Do not be deceived by the largeness of the world and the smallness of you. I see not as the world sees, and I reward not as the world rewards."

I don't know what those rewards will be. The Scriptures reveal very little of what they are in tangible terms. But if God rewards anything like He creates, I'm confident it will be overwhelming.

3. We will reign with Him.

Another promise in Scripture relates to this eternal perspective: "To him who overcomes I will grant to sit with Me on My throne, as I also overcame and sat down with My Father on His throne."[3] Paul also mentions this promise in his second letter to Timothy, the one he wrote just before Paul's own death. "If we endure, we shall also reign with Him."[4]

When I look at what is happening in the world, I am tempted to despair of God ever getting the reverence and recognition He deserves. The world is so full of despots and dictators and people who have attained power and then used it for greed and destruction. All the scandals in Congress go to show us these abuses even take place in our own nation.

But then I turn to these Scriptures and I realize we will have our chance. And it will last for eternity! God assures us we will reign with Him.

What does that say to the poor immigrant born in squalor who never gets out of the ghetto but who believes in Christ? What would that have said to first-century slaves who had no real hope of anything except a life of abject subservience? It was this message of hope—that this life is not the end, that our deeds are remembered and will be rewarded, and that we will reign with Christ—that set the first-century world aflame. People were galvanized. This was a message that held them. For the first time they had real hope!

Dr. Carl F. H. Henry, a foremost American theologian, said of Jesus, "He planted the only durable rumor of hope amid the widespread despair of a hopeless world."

Consider what 95 percent of the people in the world face every day: War. Famine. Hatred.

Genocide. We see in Somalia and Bosnia just a glimmer of what it is like for so many. How can people live like that? They can't. Some succumb to despair and die. Others die from natural causes. But the great mystery and joy of our faith is that we have real hope. Even if we face death and die, that is not the end for us. We will reign. Our day is coming.

4. We are going to become perfect, like Christ.

There's one more aspect of this eternal perspective. It's the fact that we're going to become perfect, holy, like Jesus Himself. There's a great truth in 1 John 3:2-3: "Beloved, now we are children of God; and it has not yet been revealed what we shall be, but we know that when He is revealed, we shall be like Him, for we shall see Him as He is. And everyone who has this hope in Him purifies himself, just as He is pure."

How many times have I lamented my proneness to mistakes and sins? How often I've wished I was perfect.

Well, one day each of us will be. We'll be with Him forever, and we'll be like Him in character. God has promised that "He who has begun a good work in you will complete it until the day of Jesus Christ."[5] We'll never sin again. We'll never again make the kind of mistakes that really hurt us or others. We'll never harm another person or be around people who could harm us. We'll worship and fellowship and love and give and share in perfection forever and ever.

We'll never speak another harsh, cutting word.

We'll never commit another painful, mean act.

We'll never think another prejudiced, evil thought.

We'll be perfect.

I'll even be able to eat whatever I want! No more diabetic diet for me!

How long?

Forever?

5. We will live forever.

It's said that if the world became a giant steel ball and one lone sparrow walked all around it day after day at a sparrow's pace, the first morning of eternity would still have only just begun when that sparrow had worn that ball into two halves!

Going through hard times, enduring a financial blowout, living through the death of a spouse or friend, persevering through the excruciating pain of cancer or AIDS, all of that can seem like an eternity in itself. But the apostle Paul looked at it correctly. He said, "For I consider that the sufferings of this present time are not worthy to be compared with the glory which shall be revealed in us."[6] With all Paul suffered, and certainly he suffered as much as any of us, he could keep an upbeat, fervent, hopeful outlook because he saw eternity on the horizon. He knew no matter how bad it was in the present, one day it would pass and he'd be with his Lord in heaven forever.

John Todd, a nineteenth-century minister, lost both his parents when he was six years old. He lived with a loving aunt until he left home to study for the ministry. Years later, the aunt fell ill and in great distress wrote him a letter in which she said, "I fear death is the end of everything." This is the letter Todd wrote in response to his beloved aunt's cry for hope:

> It is not thirty-five years since I, as a boy of six, was left quite alone in the world. You sent me word you would give me a home and be a kind mother to me. I have never forgotten the day I made the long journey to your house. I can recall my disappointment when, instead of coming for me yourself, you sent your servant, Caesar, to fetch me.
>
> I remember my tears and anxiety as, perched high on your horse and clinging tight to Caesar, I rode off to my new home. Night fell before we finished the journey, and I became lonely and afraid. "Do you think she'll go to bed before we get there?" I asked Caesar. "Oh no!" he said reassuringly, "She'll stay up for you. When we get out o' these here woods, you'll see her candle shinin' in the window."
>
> Presently we did ride out into the clearing, and there, sure enough, was your candle. I remember

you were waiting at the door, that you put your arms close about me—a tired and bewildered little boy. You had a fire burning on the hearth, a hot supper waiting on the stove. After supper you took me to my new room, heard me say my prayers, and then sat beside me till I fell asleep.

Someday soon God will send for you, to take you to a new home. Don't fear the summons, the strange journey, or the messenger of death. God can be trusted to do as much for you as you were kind enough to do for me so many years ago. At the end of the road you will find love and welcome awaiting, and you will be safe in God's care.[7]

There is one set of odds that none of us will beat, and that is the odds against dying. Unless we live in the generation that is raptured before death and "meet the Lord in the air," we will all face "the final frontier." Only one time in history has death been permanently scuttled. That was at the resurrection of Christ. Death is the ultimate surety, the one thing we can all count on. (That, and taxes, I suppose).

In the end, my parents and many of my friends have succumbed to death. The odds beat them. And no matter how fervent a battle I have waged against diabetes, the odds will also beat me. And you.

If death is the end, the odds cannot be beaten. If there is no afterlife, no eternity, the odds are infinity to one. None of us can overcome them.

But that is the beauty of the Christian faith. Death is not the end. The odds are not against us. We can beat them in Christ. Paul told the Thessalonians not to grieve at the deaths of their friends "as others who have no hope" because a day would come when the dead are raised and we "meet the Lord in the air."[8] He told the Corinthians, "Behold, I tell you a mystery: We shall not all sleep, but we shall all be changed—in a moment, in the twinkling of an eye, at the last trumpet. For the trumpet will sound, and the dead will be raised incorruptible, and we shall be changed."

Paul concluded the passage, "'Death is swallowed up in victory. O Death, where is your sting? O Hades, where is your victory?' The sting of death is sin, and the strength of sin is the law. But thanks be to God, who gives us the victory through our Lord Jesus Christ."[9] We shall overcome. We shall beat the odds!

The movie *City of Hope* portrays a disillusioned young doctor named Max who leaves a hospital in the United States to take a long leave of absence from life. While sightseeing in Calcutta, he is robbed and ends up meeting an older nurse who ministers to the down-and-outers of that sprawling city in a small, charity-supported clinic. He also meets a middle-aged Indian named Asari who is trying desperately to support his family by pulling rickshaw cabs all day and into the night. He first works for the powerful business overlord who owns all the cab business in that area. But eventually Asari is fired because he speaks out against his employer's evil practices.

Through the help of his friends, Asari gets his own rickshaw and starts his own business. In the process, Max and Asari go up against the powerful underworld forces who threaten to destroy them and the clinic. In the end, they win in a court battle that turns their world upside down.

After this battle, Max and Asari walk off into the city, happy victors and close, intimate friends. Max has found his calling. Asari has discovered dignity in his work and a way to meet his family's needs. Asari says to Max, "The gods haven't made it easy to be a human being."

Max replies, "I guess that's what makes it so . . . wonderful to beat the odds."

I hope you will beat the odds against you in the days ahead. Remember, you have a Lord who has called you to heaven. In the end, no odds can beat you because He has beaten them all from the start.

Epilogue

A Man from Arkansas

A story that inspired me in my quest to meet the odds is about a young country man, a beautiful young lady, and an old mongrel dog. I'd like to close this book with that tale, which changed my life.

A strange young man, raised in rural Arkansas, as I was, had never been more than thirty miles from home. He met and subsequently married a beautiful young lady. Together they purchased the first member of their new family: a huge, red mongrel dog they called Boy Dog. They settled on their farm and began to prosper; they even had the hope of replacing their three-room bungalow with a new farmhouse. Then the Second World War erupted, and the young man, like thousands of others, had to go. His wife, his mongrel dog, and his dad (the mother had passed on years before) took him to the train about thirty miles away.

Time and time again in the next few years the young man would beat the odds. On the Leyte landing in the Philippines, 125 went in, but only 25 walked out. He was one of the 25. Once he sat in a secure foxhole but just felt he ought to move. He did, and moments later the foxhole was blown up. Under all the pressure, one of his buddies went insane. He was sent to help the man, and as he was bending over to pick up some supplies, a sudden instinct told him to turn quickly. He interrupted a knife headed for his back and overcame the attacker. Six hundred and twenty-five went out in his company. Only three of the original crew members came back—he was one of the three.

Meanwhile, back home the young wife longed for her husband. She wrote him:

Dearest Husband,

I have thrilling, wonderful news. I am expecting a baby come late March. You'll be a papa. I saw Dr. Fox this week and he said that was what those sick spells I've been having were all about. I can't tell you how happy I am and how much I wish you to be here with me.

I fear for you greatly, and Boy Dog must, too, for the other night after I had gone to bed he raised up the most lonesome howl I've ever before heard. I've never known him to howl and the sound was awesome, sending chills up and down my spine. He was wet from the rain, but I let him come into the house and from that night on he has slept on the floor by my bed. When I cook for myself I also cook enough for Boy Dog. He is so much company to me with you being so far away.

I had to sell Gin and Doll and the cattle, as they were getting too much for me to take care of with the winter coming on. Gin didn't seem to mind, but Doll really threw a fit, and I had to leave the window as the men loaded her.

Mama stays here with me part of the time. Don't worry about me; just take care of yourself and be thinking of a name for the baby. May God be with you.

> Love,
> Your Wife,
> Dollie

Back home Boy Dog roamed the countryside, searching for his master in one small town after another. In his search, he would have one dogfight after another—somehow always surviving.

At last the war in the Philippines was over and the young man headed on to Japan and almost certain death. Then one day the captain told the company, "Now hear this! Now hear this! The war has ended. The Japanese have unconditionally surrendered."

One could hear a pin drop. Then the repetition

came. "Now hear this! Now hear this! The war has ended. The Japanese have unconditionally surrendered."

This time the message was clear. Pandemonium broke out with great shouts of joy. The young man from Arkansas was going home to his young wife, his precious new baby, and yes, to Boy Dog. He had beaten the odds!

The soldier tells of his return in his own words:

After three days in San Francisco, I found myself on a southern-bound train headed for Arkansas. I arrived in Little Rock and continued my journey on to Blytheville with a buddy of mine. As I stepped off the train, I thought of how this was the very spot where I'd said my farewells an eternity ago, it seemed to me.

I made my way to the outskirts of town. With my army pack on my back, I was going to try my luck at hitch-hiking the remaining twenty miles.

As I stood there beside the edge of the highway, a car began slowing down to stop. The man inside rolled down the window and said, "Get in, soldier!" Then he looked over at me again. "Well, well, Ike, is that you?"

It was Mr. Kennett, a man I knew from Leachville. We shook hands and he tried to catch me up on all the news from home.

"You know, Ike," he said, "that big, red dog of yours has been seen all over this country! He's been

seen in town and at practically all the neighbors'
houses, especially when you and your wife were
both gone. Looking for you, I suppose. Everybody
just seemed to watch out for him. I suppose the
folks here at home thought they might be helping
you out in the war, in some small way, by looking
out for him. He'd stay somewhere a day or so and
then move on. He's quite a dog."

"Yes, that he most certainly is," I replied. "Thanks
for looking out for him and thanks for the ride," I
said, as we approached the road that led from the
highway to my house.

"Don't you want me to run you on down to your
house?" he asked.

"If you don't mind, Mr. Kennett, I'd rather just
walk from here. Thanks again for the ride. Good-
bye."

It was the twenty-eighth day of December, 1945,
and there was a chill in the morning air as I stepped
out of his car and onto the dirt road—the dirt road
that led home.

As I stood there buttoning up my overcoat, I
looked toward my house and then over toward
Papa's house. I wondered how he was feeling today.
Dollie had said that he hadn't been feeling well
lately. I looked at the stalks left standing there in Mr.
Moore's cotton field and I wondered if he'd had a
good crop this year.

I felt the anticipation growing inside as I picked
up my bag and started walking, knowing that

shortly I'd be seeing my daughter and my wife. This was the day I'd dreamed of, night after night, as I'd laid in the foxholes. I almost had to pinch myself to realize that I was no longer dreaming.

A little over halfway, where the tall cottonwood stood, I could see the house in full view. I stopped and whistled, wondering if Boy Dog would hear. I watched as he raised his head in a curious manner from where he lay resting on the old meat block. At first he didn't move, but his ears were standing upright and he was watching me.

I whistled again. This time he bounded off the front porch onto the frozen earth and here he came! He had remembered the whistle! He knew who I was!

I dropped my bag and knelt down on one knee as he came closer. "Here, Boy," I said, observing his actions closely. No human face could have shown more emotion than did Boy Dog's. As I put my arms around his mighty neck, I felt his old heart pounding heavily and I noticed the streaks of gray that were mingled in among the red. Boy Dog had become an old dog. The years had taken their toll and he had aged greatly in the four years that I'd been away.

"I'm home, fellow," I said. "You don't have to go out looking anymore. I'm home to stay."

He barked as if to say he understood what I was saying.

"Now, Boy Dog, let's you and me get on toward

the house. I've been looking forward to this day for a long time and, by the way, fellow, I think that you've got somebody to introduce me to, haven't you?"

The story above shows how, time after time, God did protect me and how, with Him, I beat the odds. He was there. He did care.

A couple of years after I returned home, Boy Dog died. But by then I was blessed with a son. I wish I could have spared him some of the trials he would have to face, but then that wasn't God's way. I guess I should have known that God would have to lead my son through trials, too. It was all in His perfect plan.[1]

These words altered my life forever—words that told of Ike Minirth, my father, my older sister, and Boy Dog, all friends who taught me how to beat the odds!

Notes

Chapter 2. The Vine and the Branches

1. John 15:5.
2. John 15:7.
3. John 14:12.
4. Philippians 4:13.
5. Psalm 33:10.
6. Proverbs 16:4.
7. Ephesians 1:11.
8. Romans 8:28.
9. See Acts 4:11-12 and Hebrews 11:5-6.
10. Acts 17:26-28.
11. Acts 14:15-17.
12. Matthew 7:7.
13. Anthony Robbins, *Awaken the Giant Within* (New York: Simon and Schuster, 1991), 73.
14. Matthew 28:20, Hebrews 13:5, and Proverbs 3:5.
15. 2 Timothy 4:7.
16. Matthew 28:19-20.
17. Dick Eastman, *No Easy Road* (Grand Rapids, Mich.: Baker, 1971), 19.

18. My paraphrase of 2 Timothy 3:16-17.
19. John 15:7
20. Proverbs 16:3.

Chapter 3. The Triangle of Power

1. Hebrews 11:3.
2. Hebrews 4:12.
3. Herbert Vander Lugt, "The Power of God's Word," *Our Daily Bread,* 20 April 1983.
4. Herbert Vander Lugt, "Testify with Tact," *Our Daily Bread,* 22 July 1981.
5. Sergei Kourdakov, *The Persecutor* (Old Tappan, N.J.: Revell, 1973), 219.
6. Robbins, *Awaken the Giant Within,* 181.
7. 2 Peter 3:18.
8. James Montgomery Boice, *The Sovereign God* (Downer's Grove, Ill.: InterVarsity Press, 1979), 57-58.
9. E. M. Bounds, *Power Through Prayer* (Grand Rapids, Mich.: Zondervan, 1962), 71.
10. Dick Eastman, *No Easy Road* (Grand Rapids, Mich.: Baker, 1971), 22.
11. James M. Boice, *Philippians: An Expositional Commentary* (Grand Rapids, Mich.: Zondervan, 1982), 276-77.
12. Judges 6:37.

Chapter 4. The Total Person

1. Quoted in *Bits and Pieces,* a publication of the Economics Press, Fairfield, New Jersey, March 1979.
2. Colossians 3:25.
3. Galatians 6:7.

4. Romans 6:23.
5. 2 Thessalonians 2:3.
6. Proverbs 23:7.
7. 1 Peter 4:8.
8. Matthew 5:44 and Romans 12:19.
9. 1 John 4:18.
10. Quoted in *Reader's Digest,* December 1981.
11. Matthew 6:14–15.
12. David Augsburger, *The Freedom of Forgiveness* (Grand Rapids, Mich.: Zondervan, 1970), 39.
13. James 5:16.
14. Acts 1:8.
15. Matthew 28:19.

Chapter 5. The Palm of His Hand

1. Hebrews 13:5.
2. 1 Corinthians 6:19.
3. Romans 8:16.
4. Romans 8:14–15.
5. Henry G. Bosch, *Our Daily Bread.*
6. Philippians 4:6–7.
7. 2 Corinthians 1:8.
8. John 16:33.
9. Philip Yancey, *Where Is God When It Hurts?* (Grand Rapids, Mich.: Zondervan, 1989).
10. Billy Graham, *Angels: God's Secret Agents* (New York: Doubleday, 1975), 3.
11. Norman Vincent Peale, *The Power of Positive Thinking* (New York: Prentice-Hall, 1952).
12. From *The Christian Reader*, 10 September 1979.
13. Ephesians 2:10.

14. Psalm 139:14.
15. Exodus 14:13.

Chapter 6. The Turning Tide

1. Psalm 3:6, 1 Corinthians 15:58, Ephesians 6:10, and Ephesians 6:13.
2. Quoted in *Reader's Digest,* September 1978.
3. *Reader's Digest,* December 1983, 194.
4. Colossians 3:23–24.
5. Quoted in *Christianity Today,* 25 May 1979.
6. Acts 10:9–13.

Chapter 7. The Ultimate Victory

1. Romans 5:3–5.
2. Philippians 1:12–14.
3. 1 Thessalonians 3:2–4.
4. John 15:5.
5. Philippians 1:6.
6. Quoted in *Reader's Digest,* October 1980.
7. 2 Corinthians 12:9–10.

Chapter 8. The Eternal Perspective

1. Colossians 3:23–24.
2. Matthew 10:42.
3. Revelation 3:21.
4. 2 Timothy 2:12.
5. Philippians 1:6.
6. Romans 8:18.
7. Vernon Grounds, "Death," *Leadership,* Spring 1987, 52.

8. 1 Thessalonians 4:13, 17.
9. 1 Corinthians 15:51–52, 54–57.

Epilogue. A Man from Arkansas

1. This is my father's story. His manuscript was first printed in *Beating the Odds* by Frank Minirth, Ike Minirth with Georgia Minirth Beach, and Mary Alice Minirth (Grand Rapids, Mich.: Baker, 1987), 25–41.